The Dogma and the Triumph

The Dogma and the Triumph

Mark I. Miravalle, S.T.D.

Foreword by Luis Cardinal Aponte Martínez,
Archbishop of San Juan, Puerto Rico

Queenship

PUBLISHING COMPANY
P.O Box 42028 Santa Barbara, CA 93140-2028
(800) 647-9882 • (805) 957-4893 • Fax: (805) 957-1631

IMPRIMATUR:
Bernardino Cardinal Echeverría Ruiz, O.F.M.
Archbishop Emeritus of Guayaquil
Apostolic Administrator of Ibarra
Solemnity of the Mother of God
1 January 1998

©1998 Queenship Publishing Company

Library of Congress #: 98-65192

Published by:
Queenship Publishing
P.O. Box 42028
Santa Barbara, CA 93140-2028
(800) 647-9882 • (805) 957-4893 • Fax: (805) 957-1631

Printed in the United States of America

ISBN: 1-57918-067-1

Contents

Dedication

To the Sacred and Immaculate Hearts of Jesus and Mary:

May the Triumph of the Immaculate Heart of Mary, initiated by the solemn definition of Our Lady Coredemptrix, Mediatrix, and Advocate, prepare all hearts for the Reign of the Most Sacred and Eucharistic Heart of Jesus, all by the power of the Holy Spirit, for the glory of the Heavenly Abba, the Father of all Mankind.

Foreword

Let us go and adore Christ the Redeemer who has wished us to have everything that is good through Mary.

With these words of the old invitation to matins of the feast dedicated to Mary, Mediatrix of all graces, we participate in this encounter whose solemnity we celebrate and which represents the gift to humanity of Christ to the world, formed in the body of his blessed Mother, Mary of Nazareth. This event is related to the gift of freedom granted to man, which is one of the names which the fundamental grace of Redemption may have: "In order for us to be free, we were made free by Christ," and associated, by divine decree, is the woman who has the title of Co-Redemptrix. This coredemptive role is witnessed in diverse manners since the ancient analogies of the Fathers, like St. Irenaeus in the second century, when he established a radical and antithetical parallelism between the old and the new Eve, who upon associating herself to the husband of the New Alliance, and one unique decree, in the feeling and sayings of the Franciscan school, so sensitive and intuitive of the Marian privileges, desired by God, has made her Mother of the new human beings.

And when she Co-Redeemed with her Son by participating with Him in the only Redemption which He merits for man, it also becomes a source of freedom and liberation within the mission of her Son, according to the words quoted from Galatians (cf. Gal 4:4-6). This gift of freedom in which in a special manner we can see the hand of God when He makes man in his own image is not easily shown to a mind deviated by the superficiality or by the incorrect relationship between the same freedom and the truth which measure that freedom and makes it possible, because "only that freedom which submits itself to the truth may take that person to the true good." "The goodness of the person consists of being in the truth and living the truth." In light of the contemporary difficulties of understanding the profound meaning of the true sense of freedom, the splendor of the truth in Christ, crucified and resurrected, shines before our eyes in His free sacrificial oblation to the Father and for His brothers: "Christ crucified reveals the authentic meaning of freedom, He lives freedom fully in the total gift of Himself and calls His disciples to take part of His own freedom" (*Veritatis Splendor*, 85).

In fact, "The contemplation of Jesus crucified is the master road through which the Church must walk every day if it wishes to understand the full meaning of freedom: the giving of oneself at the service of God and his own brothers." This free giving of Himself in His Passion in favor of all mankind freely accepted is advanced in the Last Supper when He institutes the

Eucharistic Mystery of the Body and the Blood of Our Lord: "Take and eat, this is my body which shall be delivered for you." To the oblational love of that Last Supper, the full freedom in which it is given and the freedom-redemption for which it is given, make that Eucharist the center of the Incarnation and of the union of freedom and grace. It is a shining synthesis which merges the unique decree wherein the Son "born of a woman" unites in an extraordinary manner the divine condescendence which attracts man like a collaborator in the greatest work of creation, which is the Redemption of Jesus Christ.

In that collaboration we can see one of the variables of the human being, "male and female He created them," the feminine part, the woman indissolubly raised to the freedom and ready made grace until She becomes, through the deed and the grace of the Most Holy Spirit, the course through which the Son of God, He who is life itself, descends to earth. "I am the way, the truth and the life," and He does it through the only road chosen by Divine design and by no other in the present economy who gives Him the body, the soul and who with her Fiat allows the Person of the only Son of the Father to lovingly and joyfully flow through Her person, "He Who is full of grace and of truth," thus fulfilling the divine maternity.

This is our faith, the faith of the Church. And according to this faith, sometimes explicitly, with implications which our reason illuminated by the coherence of that same faith clarifies on other occasions, it is deduced with a great transparency in theological certainty what the Holy tradition of the Church illuminates since the beginning of this truth, getting insights from the depths of the Church's history of thoughts up to the nearest in the statements of the Ecclesiastical Magisterium. In the mid part of the eighteenth century Pope Benedict XIV in his Bull *Gloriosae Dominae*, very clearly and unequivocally proclaims that "She (Mary) is like a heavenly river through whom all divine graces and gifts flow to the miserable mortals." After Pope Benedict XIV, all the other Popes, up to the present Pope John Paul II in his Encyclical Letter *Redemptoris Mater*, speak of Mary's association in the unique mediation of Jesus Christ, and resonate the doctrine set by the Fathers of the Second Vatican Council on the action of the Mother of the Redeemer in the Church. This represents the mouth of a great river which, from the primary source has been collecting all waters until it reaches the ocean, in this case the stated and unequivocal deposit of the Catholic Faith.

Has the hour arrived in which the encounter of the river of this Marian belief with the ocean of the faith of the people of God can request the Holy Father to offer this same people the dogmatic certainty of a truth which illustrates the unique and central fact of the life of the Church and of human history, the Incarnation of the Son of God and the beginning of the only liberation which man, and with him the entire creation, reaches with the Redemption of Jesus Christ?

Because the same Church, in fidelity to itself and to the Revelation entrusted to the same, may easily find that this truth of the universal mediation of the Mother of God, is not the circumstantial product of an isolated impulse of a fleeting feeling that has very little to do with the prior faith of the Church. The serious research in regards to the Church Fathers of the first centuries, which today represent for the scholars a conquest of difficult debate, takes us closer to the richness of that new born spring. For example, in the second century with Bishop St. Irenaeus, witness of the ecclesiastic faith in so many points, proclaimed very probably the opinion of his contemporaries, when, after establishing the antithesis Eve-Mary, concludes by saying that Mary came to be by her obedience the obedient Virgin, *restorem* of what the disobedient virgin, Eve, had undone, untying with the Virgin Mary's faith what the virgin Eve had tied with her incredulity. The same ideas are found substantially in authors so early as St. Justin, St. Epiphanius, St. Ambrose, St. Jerome, St. Augustine, St. Peter Christologos and others who transmit and slowly spread the existing faith about this Marian privilege.

And in this way the title of Mediatrix so frequently applied to Our Lady in the following centuries resonates for the first time, towards those first times. It seems it was St. Ephraem, the Syrian, the first one who used that word, before the end of the fourth century, in reference to the Mother of God: "To Thee do I come, Mediatrix of the entire world, I invoke your protection in my needs." St. Cyril of Jerusalem, in the fifth century, says in a homily he read in the presence of the Bishops gathered in Ephesus in 431: "That (Mary) from whom the devils flee in fear, by whom the fallen creature is raised to the heavens." And we could close the third century with the beautiful words of an *Encomium* attributed to St. Modest of Jerusalem, but more probably written in the latter part of the year 600: "Mankind has been saved by you, and by you mankind has received unending favors and blessings from Him (God)."

From the eighth to the eighteenth century wherein they start resolute invocation to the Mother of God as Mediatrix of all graces with Pope Benedict XIV, the history of the Church and the Sacred Tradition continue advancing slow and solemnly in the affirmations of theologians in communion with the Catholic faith, as well as the Doctors and Saints who seize this truth of the *sensus fidei*, of the people of God. At the same time they strengthen the same with theological reasons and liturgical practices. The liturgies of the Orient, the Byzantine, the Coptic, the Syriac, the Armenian and the Chaldean, present beautiful and direct texts which support this same faith. In the Latin liturgy we would mention the institution of the festivity.

In closer times, on behalf of Pope Benedict XV in the year 1921 of Mary, Mediatrix of all graces for the religious orders and of the dioceses who might request the same and which should be celebrated on the last day of the month of May.

And thus we can say, in synthesis, that the waters of the teachings of tradition and the liturgical celebrations coincide making truth, once again, the illuminating theological principle "lex orandi, lex credendi." Certainly there is no doubt that this argumental richness of the *intellectum quarens fidem* starts from the so-called protogospel of the text of Genesis: "I shall place enmity between you and the Woman, between your descendants and Her descendants." The before mentioned antithetical parallelism of the Fathers of the second century, Eve-Ave, places the Mother of God at the origin of the life-grace founder of the new salvific economy when she begot Her Son, Jesus of Nazareth, true God and true man, in front of the mother of all humans, Eve, who placed herself at the beginning of the disgrace of mankind for having listened to and accepted the word from the Fallen Angel and having given her yes to its fatal Catechesis. A legitimate structural reading of the alluded literary text presents the Virgin Mary, Mother of God, at the beginning of all grace, when she gave her consent to the Heavenly Angel who proclaims Her divine maternity. The betrothal of the New Eve to the Holy Spirit inaugurates a new and definitive historical order whose doors are opened by Mary.

That obedience to the action of the Spirit makes the human variable of man, that is the feminine part, frustrated in Eve, come intimately closer to the substantial saintliness of the Father and the Son, which is the Holy Spirit of Love, Lord and Giver of Life

(Creed in Mass) because God is Love. And so, the Spirit Grantor of Life, He who is the Life of the World, is splendidly manifested in the creature He has begotten, the Theotokos, because the maternal statute of Mary transcends what is merely biological to integrate it in the moral order of human freedom, which is the environment of the responsible and interpersonal consequences taken in this case to a yes of a co-redemption which arises from a unique divine decree in the Incarnation, of the free character of the Redeemer going to His Passion "voluntarily accepted" (Eucharistic Prayer II) and of the yes of the Virgin of Nazareth who has freely accepted the order of Incarnation and Redemption, to which She is now associated by God in Her own liberty. *To separate Mary's co-redemption from the redemption of Jesus Christ is to separate what God has united.* This is so clear to a theologian who represents the best Marian sensibility today that he has no doubts in stating with the responsibility and character he is famous for, that "any deviation of this doctrine (about the mediation born out of the co-redemption) would threaten the integrity of the Faith."

The New Testament, especially the Fourth Gospel, so symbolic and allusive, that is, with trends that unite the expression of the human language and the contents of Divine Revelation. This truth is referred to in the stories of the Wedding at Cana and in the Passion and Pentecost, opening roads of acceptance of this doctrine very coherent before this grace granted to the Mediatrix of all graces through eminent means. Because when She gave us the first and the source of all other graces, Jesus of Nazareth, Son of God, begotten by Mary, She gives us all gifts together with Him.

The cautions in announcing this Marian privilege, which only the charity in the truth shall set the hour of the deep confrontations between the separated brethren and the Catholic Church, should not lose sight of the prudent discernment in regards to an authentic ecumenism which is not shy in proclaiming what is very clear for tradition, source of revelation. Because if we hesitate it would only lead us to disregard the integrity of the teachings relative to the great theologians of protest who know and assume the great real differences still remaining between them and us, and which lie precisely in the fundamental fact of the Incarnation of a God which becomes man in a mysterious descent, and this is essential to identify what is catholic. That is the knot which with all due respect, but with the courage of the truth which makes us free, we have to say it has not been cut.

We are a few years away to commemorate the two thousand years of this event that has reordered the human adventure full of so many successes and so many tears, making it enter into the final stage of the salvation, of the liberation and of the definitive fulfillment, even though it is just incoated of man. Would we be out of line in our wishes if we were to say that the honor of the Father, the honor of the Son Incarnate and the honor of the Holy Spirit, who infused the grace of divine maternity in the Virgin of Nazareth, that the honor of the Mother of God and the splendor of the truth of Her universal mediation of all graces, founded upon her role as Coredemptrix, so lived since ancient times by the sense of the faith of the Christian people redeemed and co-redeemed by the Son and the Mother, were asking in a coherent manner for the solemn and infallible explanation in the commemorative year of the Incarnation that we are about to celebrate?

In ardent hope, brothers, let us wish and pray to heaven that this salvific Marian truth may shine for the glory of God, for the praise of the Mother of the Church and our salvation.

> Luis Cardinal Aponte Martínez
> Archbishop of San Juan
> 8 December 1997
> Solemnity of the Immaculate Conception

Introduction

This small booklet consists of an edited transcription of a trilogy of oral reflections delivered in Rome during the *Vox Populi Mariae Mediatrici* International Leaders Conference, May 30-31, 1997. Present at the Conference were over fifty Cardinals and Bishops representative of the six continents, as well as theologians, religious, priests and lay leaders spanning some forty countries.

This meeting of "lovers of Our Lady's heart," truly a great cross section of Church hierarchy and laity alike, were assembled in prayer and dialogue for the advancement of the solemn papal definition of the Maternal Mediation of the Blessed Virgin Mary under the three essential aspects of Coredemptrix, Mediatrix of all Grace, and Advocate for the People of God. The *Vox Populi Mariae Mediatrici* (Voice of the People for Mary Mediatrix) international Catholic movement has gathered the prayer support and petitions of over 500 bishops, inclusive of 42 cardinals, and of nearly 5 million Catholics from 157 countries of the world in support of the papal proclamation of Our Lady's Maternal Mediation by our present *Totus Tuus* Vicar of Christ.

The overall theme of the reflections is contained in the work's title, *The Dogma and the Triumph*. "In the end, my Immaculate Heart will Triumph," (13 July 1917) so foretold the Mother of God under the title of Our Lady of the Rosary at Fatima. Mystically intertwined with the great Fatima prophesy is the proclamation of "the whole truth about Mary," the papal definition of her sanctifying action for the People of God and for the Church as the Coredemptrix ("the Mother Suffering"), the Mediatrix of all Grace ("the Mother Nourishing"), and the Advocate for all God's people ("the Mother Pleading"). It is from the realm of the greatest Christian mysteries that God the Father, in His perfect providence, so radically respects the domain of human freedom. So too is human freedom respected regarding the Dogma and the Triumph.

Until the Vicar of Christ exercises his freedom in the name of all mankind by solemnly proclaiming the truth about the salvific action of the Mother of God — our Coredemptrix, Mediatrix, and Advocate — who mediates to us "the gifts of eternal salvation" (cf. *Lumen Gentium*, n.62), then our Mother cannot exercise the full spiritual capacity of her sanctifying functions of grace and mercy for the Church and for the world. At a time in the history of the Church and the world where the inestimable graces of our redeeming Saviour are so needed, especially as we prepare for the third millennium of Christianity, so we ardently long for and do all humanly possible for the full exercise of Our Lady's profound intercessory power. How great and glorious it would be for our beloved *Totus Tuus* Pope to proclaim this whole truth about the Virgin Mother of the Church so as to give Our Lady *our fiat* to the manifestation of her full mediating and sanctifying power for us, a supernatural power of grace given to her by her Divine Son.

Full love of Mary must be based on the whole truth about Mary. The Triumph of her Immaculate Heart, the union of hearts in common love of the Immaculate Heart, remains intimately and essentially connected with the solemn papal proclamation of the full truth about her. It is my prayer and hope that these brief reflections can, in some small way, contribute to the appreciation of both mind and heart as to the quintessential importance of this Marian Dogma and its integral relation to the Triumph of the Immaculate Heart, both of which will provide supernatural preparation for the great Jubilee of the Incarnation in the year 2000.

May this family of hearts, this Marian Remnant, persevere unto Calvary with Our Lady Coredemptrix and be spiritually united to the Crucified One throughout this great work. And may their generous adoring of His Eucharistic presence in the most Blessed Sacrament, allow them to cooperate fully for the rich ecclesial fruit of the promised Era of Peace, which was also prophetically foretold at Fatima to be a time of Eucharistic Reign and recognition, a new springtime for the Church (cf. John Paul II, *Tertio Millennio Adveniente*, n.18).

Mark I. Miravalle, S.T.D.
President, *Vox Populi Mariae Mediatrici*
Professor of Theology and Mariology
Franciscan University of Steubenville
1 January 1998, *Solemnity of the Mother of God*

Chapter 1

The Papal Definition of Our Lady Coredemptrix, Mediatrix, Advocate and the Triumph of the Immaculate Heart of Mary

"The Dogma and the Triumph"

The dynamic drama of how "God saves man" as ordained in the perfect providence of the Eternal Father, He who is Father of All Mankind, is revealed in Galatians 4:4-6. Let us reflect on this passage, which our beloved Holy Father, Pope John Paul II, so often quotes in his principal Marian addresses. From the New Vulgate: *"Ubi venit plenitudo temporis, misit Filium suum factum ex muliere... ut adoptionem filiorum reciperemus. Quoniam autem estis filii, misit Deus Spiritum Filii sui in corda vestra clamantem: Abba, Pater"* ("When in the fullness of time, God sent His Son, born of a woman, so that we may be adopted sons. And because you are sons, God has sent the Spirit of His Son into our hearts, crying: 'Abba! Father!'").

This statement is St. Paul's only direct reference to the Mother of God and our own Mother Mary. Here

1

he gives us, through the power of the Holy Spirit, an unequaled summary in seven pillars of revelation concerning the entire plan of human salvation:

> *"Ubi venit plenitudo temporis."* "When, in the fullness of time."

In an authentically Marian sense, we have reached the fullness of time. We have reached that which has been called the climax of the Age of Mary, an apex, a summit, a high point that has been preceded by many holy events and great saints and teachers. We need only consider the writings of St. Maximilian Kolbe, for example, and the efforts of Cardinal Mercier of Belgium who was the first to receive, through his intercession and petitioning to Pope Benedict XV, the Mass and Office of *Mediatrix Omnium Gratiarum* (Mediatrix of all graces). Let us recall also the many theologians and the many bishops, religious, and lay people who over the centuries kept Our Lady Coredemptrix and Mediatrix of all Grace deeply within their hearts. It is because of them also that we are now privileged to be living in the climax of the Age of Mary.

Let us recall also the messages and titles of our Heavenly Mother that have been approved by the Church from such places as Rue du Bac, La Salette, Lourdes, Fatima, Beauring, Amsterdam, Akita, as well as the numerous contemporary reported Marian apparition sites. All elements of theology, faith and ecclesial life are calling us to the awareness that we have reached the climax of the Age of Mary.

Above all, we are grateful to our prophetic, heroic pontiff, Pope John Paul II. It is because of his courageous witness and leadership as the "Totus Tuus" Vicar of Christ that we can say with peace and with courage, "Yes, through no merits of our own, we are called to a great responsibility, to participation in this climax of the Age of Mary." Because he is *totally hers*, because he belongs totally to the Blessed Virgin, we must remember the unconditional requirement for participation in the Triumph of the Immaculate Heart of Mary; the *sine qua non*, is *full and complete obedience and loyalty to our Holy Father*. He is *"Petrus"* (cf. Mt: 16:15-20). He is the shepherd. We, as the sheep, must listen to his voice, and we must hear his voice. Our Lord Jesus says, "My sheep know Me, and I know Mine" (John 10:14). We must know Him *and His vicar on earth*, not only in the mind, but in the heart.

"Misit Deus Filium tuum." "God sent His Son."

The Father of all mankind initiates everything. We can never forget that the plan of salvation comes from God the Father. The Son is sent—*"missio"*. The greatest mission of human and celestial history is the sending of the Son by the Father. Too long have we neglected to focus theologically and liturgically on the Heavenly and Eternal Father from whom all things come. He is the infinite Creator and also the "Abba," which properly translated means, "Papa," "Daddy," "the Close One." We must never forget that the mercy of the Sacred Heart of Jesus, which comes to us through the Immaculate Heart of Mary, originates in the Heart of the Abba Father. The mercy of Jesus *is* the mercy of the Father. The Son is the sacrifice, the core, the center, the climax of history of heaven and earth. He is the cosmic Redeemer, the universal Redeemer, but He always acts in obedience to the Abba, Eternal Father of all.

"*Factum ex muliere*." "Born of a woman."

But this is no ordinary woman. She is *the Woman* of Genesis, the Woman of Cana, the Woman of Calvary, and the Woman of Revelation. She is above all the Woman of Redemption, who is always and in every way subordinated to the Redeemer Son. It was eternally predestined by the Father that a woman would be part of the mission of Redemption and coredemption. Pope Pius IX in his great proclaiming document, *Ineffabilis Deus*, makes it very clear that it was a singular intention of the Father both to "send his Son," and to send his Son "*factum ex muliere*," "born of a woman."

Pope John Paul II also points out in his encyclical *Redemptoris Mater*, that the Heavenly Father "entrusted himself to the Virgin of Nazareth" (n. 39). This woman was eternally and providentially designed to be a part of the plan of human salvation, not merely as a biological "host" but as an intimate partner in his mission. In our own times, when the true dignity of woman is so misunderstood, so scattered by many illusory, false concepts of woman, it is in Mary that we find the ultimate dignity of the woman, because the Father has made this woman an integral part of the plan of salvation *ab initio*, from the beginning. *This Woman* is the Father's greatest masterpiece.

All artists are sometimes called to do less than their greatest for reasons of money or occupation. All authors are sometimes called to do less than their greatest. All builders are at times called to do less than their greatest. But each should have the opportunity at least once in their life to show the full beauty, the full ability, the full power of their talents: in short, their masterpiece. The greatest masterpiece of the Abba, Father is the Woman.

Our Mother Mary was created immaculate by the Eternal Father precisely so that she could be the Coredemptrix. In the early 1970's our Holy Father, while he was still Cardinal Archbishop of Krakow, gave a beautiful address on the Feast of the Immaculate Conception. In this talk he made it very clear that Mary was created immaculate from the moment of her conception precisely so that she could be the perfect partner of Redemption with the redeeming Jesus. That which unites the Hearts of Jesus and Mary like nothing else, ontologically, is the mission of Redemption and Coredemption. Mary is the "Coredemptrix" because she was first the "Immaculate Conception."

"Ut adoptionem filiorum reciperemus."
"So that they might be adopted sons of
God."

We are born in sin. This is the fundamental human condition. And yet in our times, this truth is being lost by many. Venerable Pius XII prophetically stated that, "The greatest sin of the twentieth century is the loss of the sense of sin." If we do not know that we are in the midst of sin, then how can we see our need for a redeemer? Clear awareness of the plan of salvation is only possible when we understand our need for a redeemer, and for a coredemptrix by recognizing our own sin.

Grace is participation in the life and love of the Father, Son, and Holy Spirit. Saint Thomas Aquinas said that one baptized infant has more ontological goodness than the entire created universe put together, because that child is participating in Trinitarian life. But there is a price for this grace, there is a price in becoming adopted sons of the Father. Because there is only one true Son of God, and only one woman who is mother of that Son, it is the uncompromised historic efforts of the Redeemer and the Coredemptrix which allow us to become adopted sons. It is the Mediatrix of All Grace who brings us the graces of the Redemption, but everything starts at Calvary in the definitive battle to redeem humanity.

"Quoniam autem estis filii, misit Deus Spiritum Filii sui." "And because you are sons, God has sent the Spirit of His Son."

It is the Divine Sanctifier, the Holy Spirit, who brings us the graces of the Redemption. Saint Maximilian Kolbe tells us that the Holy Spirit acts exclusively through the Immaculata: "The union between the Immaculata and the Holy Spirit is so inexpressible, yet so perfect, that the Holy Spirit acts only by the Most Blessed Virgin, His Spouse" ("Letter to Fr. Salezy Mikolajczyk," 28 July 1935, *Immaculate Conception and the Holy Spirit*, p.99). Saint Maximilian tells us that to understand and appreciate fully the unity of the Holy Spirit and the Blessed Virgin, the Immaculata, we must look by way of analogy to the hypostatic union of Jesus Christ.

The intimate union between the Holy Spirit and Mary is comparable to the inseparable union of the divine nature and human nature in the one Divine Person of Jesus Christ. And although the Holy Spirit and Mary are two totally distinct and separate persons, and the Holy Spirit never became incarnate, nonetheless, as St. Maximilian tells us, this union is so inexpressible, so profound, that the Spirit acts only through the Bride, *not by necessity but by divine desire*, by divine disposition. And so our Mother is the Advocate, she is the human advocate who works in

7

unitate cordae, in complete unity of heart with the Divine Sanctifier, the Holy Spirit. Thus, "the Spirit and the Bride say, 'Come'" (Rev. 22:17), invoking the Lord Jesus to come at this climactic point of human history, but also to come at every moment into every human heart. The Spirit offers His divine invitation to sanctification only through the Bride, the Immaculata, who is the human instrument of the Holy Spirit. Since the Holy Spirit is Source of all grace, and Mary is His created human instrument, then, of course, the Immaculata is the Mediatrix of all graces.

"In corda vestra clamantem: Abba, Pater."
"Into our hearts, crying, 'Abba! Father!'"

The Holy Spirit under divine illumination, calls each one of us to recognize the One from whom the entire plan of salvation comes. No longer understood as the Old Testament God of justice, the Spirit reveals that the infinite mercy of the Trinity originates in the Heart of the Father. He is to be called not "omnipotence," not "omniscience," not "all-perfection," but "Abba." Thus, we should see the Heavenly Father's close, paternal love for each human child, and understand and appreciate the paternal love of the Abba for each one of us as infinitely surpassing that of the greatest of human fathers. For the Father of all mankind has the hairs of our head counted (cf. Mt 10:30). The Holy Spirit ensures that none of us forget this revealed truth. He is ever leading us back to the beginning, back to the Abba, to the Father, who is Love, who is the Paternal Originator of the entire plan of human salvation.

In summation, in Galatians 4:4-6 we have a synthesis of the divine drama of salvation, culminating in Jesus and Mary's perfect obedience to the will of the Father on Calvary. The Redeemer and the Coredemptrix lead the way. Their path of sacrificial love does not come to fruition in our lives unless we too are willing to travel to Calvary with them, opening our hearts to the graces coming from Redemption and coredemption.

Our Mother Coredemptrix at the Foot of the Cross

To imitate our Mother Coredemptrix, each one of us, each faithful, must be willing to carry our cross unto Calvary. The motto which should be emblazoned on the hearts of those consecrated to the Immaculate Heart of Mary must always be: "Mary Coredemptrix persevered unto Calvary for us. We must persevere unto Calvary for Mary Coredemptrix."

Our Mother's participation in the Redemption has been profoundly expressed by our Holy Father in his Wednesday Audience of April 2, 1997, in which he said the following about Our Lady's participation in the historic redemptive act of Jesus Christ:

"Mary joins her suffering to Jesus' priestly sacrifice. With our gaze illumined by the radiance of the Resurrection, we pause to reflect on the Mother's involvement in her Son's redeeming Passion, which was completed by her sharing in his suffering. Let us return again, but now in the perspective of the Resurrection, to the foot of the Cross, where the Mother endured 'with her only begotten Son the intensity of His suffering, associated herself with His sacrifice in her Mother's heart, and lovingly consented to the immolation of this victim which was born of her' (*Lumen Gentium*, n.58)."

"With these words, the Council reminds us of 'Mary's compassion'; in her heart reverberates all that Jesus suffers in body and soul, emphasizing her willingness to share in her Son's redeeming sacrifice and to join her own maternal suffering to his priestly offering.

"The Council text also stresses that her consent to Jesus' immolation is not passive acceptance but a genuine act of love, by which she offers her Son as a 'victim' of expiation for the sins of all humanity.

"Lastly, *Lumen Gentium* relates the Blessed Virgin to Christ, who has the lead role in Redemption, making it clear that in associating herself 'with his sacrifice' she remains subordinate to her divine Son.

"...Mary's hope at the foot of the Cross contains *a light stronger than the darkness that reigns in many hearts*: in the presence of the redeeming Sacrifice, the hope of the Church and of humanity is born in Mary" (*L'Osser-vatore Romano*, Wednesday Audience of 2 April, p.11, 9 April English edition, emphasis mine).

In his Wednesday Audience of April 9th, 1997, the Holy Father further elucidates:

"Mary's co-operation is unique and unre-peatable. However, applied to Mary, the term 'co-operator' acquires a specific meaning. The collaboration of Christians in salvation takes place after the Calvary event, whose fruits they endeavor to spread by prayer and sacrifice. Mary, instead, co-operated during the event itself and in the role of mother; thus her co-operation embraces the whole of Christ's saving work. She alone was associated in this way with the redemptive sacrifice that merited the salvation of all mankind. In union with the Christ and in submission to him, she collaborated in obtaining the

grace of salvation for all humanity"
(*L'Osservatore Romano*, p.7, 16 April English edition).

Not only is our Mother the Mediatrix of all grace, distributing the grace of Calvary, but the Pope tells us here that she also (and first of all) *participates* sacrificially in the event, she actively participates in the acquisition of the graces of the Redemption. In the obtaining of the graces of Calvary as the New Eve with the New Adam, she takes an intimate part in what has been called "objective redemption." She is Mediatrix of all grace because she is first the Coredemptrix.

To reject the gift of Mary Coredemptrix is to reject the final gift of the crucified Lord to each human heart. Why do many have difficulty accepting this gift? We are living in a time of great confusion, and thus some think that to speak the whole truth about Mary is a violation of authentic Catholic ecumenism. I would say in the most explicit terms that in order *to be fully ecumenical we must be fully Marian*. *It is only through the full truth about the Mother that we find the foundation for ultimate Christian unity.*

During times of doubt we can hear the words of the Savior saying to us, and saying to our separated brothers and sisters from Calvary, "It is I who give you my Mother. It is I" (cf. Jn 19:26). The gift of Mary's motherhood comes from the merciful heart of the Crucified, and it is given to every single human being. This is not a gift initiated by the Mother; it is initiated by our Savior himself.

The gift of the Precious Body, Blood, Soul and Divinity of Jesus, which is also the gift that comes to fruition at Calvary, is intimately united to Our Lady Coredemptrix, because His Precious Blood is also her own. His Precious Blood was given to Him by the Mother; the Hearts of Jesus and Mary were first united in the womb of the Mother, when the blood from the Immaculate Heart was pumped to her womb where the Heart of Jesus was formed. From the blood of the Immaculate Heart came the human, incarnate Heart of Jesus Christ, *in utero*. "The Word became flesh and dwelt among us..." (Jn 1:14). His flesh is formed entirely from Mary's flesh. And thus, the precious gift of the Eucharist, our Lord's very Body and blood, in which is found the Heart of Christ, is made possible to us only through the mediation of Mary. The gifts of the Eucharist and our Lady Coredemptrix are in a real sense inseparable.

In the great 15th century work *The Imitation of Christ* by Thomas á Kempis, the meditations are expressed in the first person singular, as if Jesus is speaking directly to the heart of the reader. In similar fashion, we could well hear the words of Our Lord saying to each human heart:

"Abandon yourselves to Me, into My hands, commend your spirit and I shall present you to My Father in Heaven. Do

13

not hold back any part of yourselves; trust Me. I am your Lord and Savior. I am the strength of your life. You will not die if you die to yourself, but I shall give you everlasting life. Take My Body and My Blood, and join with Me in Eternal Union. Feel My presence within you and be joyful. Look for My presence in others and join with them in fellowship, for I am with you all always. Do not despair, but rejoice, for I am with you. Remember My Passion, that I suffered for mankind; do not let it be in vain. Come to the foot of My Cross and stand with My Mother. Listen to her, take comfort from her, let her be your guide. Keep her company at the foot of My Cross, she is waiting there for you always with open arms. Come to Me, I wait for You."

When our spiritual life is in our own hands, there is peril. When our spiritual life is in the hands of the Sacred Heart of Jesus there is security, sustenance, and strength. We should never fear to make this offering of ourselves to Him. The early martyrs knew that even life itself was an appropriate offering to the Eucharistic Jesus—He who had given His Body and Blood for them. They understood that the offering of their bodies, if necessary, was a sacrifice appropriate for the greater glory of God. They understood, in the heart of their souls, the eternal fruit and real crown of accepting death for life; of losing their life so as to find it; of the dimness of the temporal compared with the brilliant light of the eternal. The eternal crown to martyrdom is of the greatest honors in the Heavenly Jerusalem, which knows no end. So too, we are called to the altar of sacrifice for our Eucharistic Jesus, for our Mother Coredemptrix, for our Holy Father, and for the glory of the Church. If the early martyrs knew that this cause was worthy of bodily sacrifice as well as spiritual sacrifice, we too must have the same conviction of heart. We must have the spirituality of Saint Ignatius of Antioch, who was willing to become flesh, who was willing to become "God's wheat, ground by the teeth of beasts, that I may be found pure bread" (*Letter to the Romans*).

In Saint John's Gospel Jesus tells us, "He who eats My flesh and drinks My blood shall have life eternal, and I will raise him up on the last day" (Jn 6:53-54). In the Eucharist we experience a foretaste of the great era that is promised, the Era of Peace, the Eucharistic era. Through this sacrament we are enabled to recognize the Eucharistic presence in one another, even in the interior tabernacles of our heart. This is true unity. This is authentic ecumenism. As the early Church knew, there is no full Christianity without coming to the Eucharistic sacrifice and partaking of the Eucharistic banquet as one, a manifestation of the full unity of faith.

Our Mother Coredemptrix is always at the foot of the cross, and she is always present with us spiritually at every tabernacle, where her Son awaits us in silence. If Our Lady is at the foot of the cross, then Our Lady's family, Our Lady's co-hearts, Our Lady's remnant, must have the courage to go and join her at the foot of the cross. This remnant may be great in numbers or small, but we must remember that on Calvary only a handful of disciples gathered with Mary and the beloved disciple. Our task is not to count numbers, but to be faithful.

Scripture tells us in Revelation 12:17: "Then the dragon was angry with the woman, and went off to make war on the remnant, on those who keep the commandments of God and bear testimony to Jesus."

Saint Paul writes in Romans 9:27: "And Isaiah cries out concerning Israel: 'Though the number of the sons of Israel be as the sand of the sea, only a remnant of them will be saved.'"

And in Romans 11:5: "So, too, at the present time there is a remnant, chosen by grace."

The prophet Zechariah tell us: "For there shall be a sowing of peace; the vine shall yield its fruit, and the ground shall give its increase, and the heavens shall give their due; and I will cause the remnant of this people to possess all things" (Zechariah 8:12).

And the prophet Micah says, "I will surely gather all of you, O Jacob. I will gather the remnant of Israel; I will set them together like sheep in a fold, like a flock in its pasture, a noisy multitude of men" (Micah 2:12).

Our Mother Coredemptrix calls her remnant to gather at the foot of the cross. In this, we must return, grasp, and benefit from the rich spirituality of the early Church which well understood that martyrdom, in both forms of white (spiritual) and red (physical) martyrdom, was a real and present aspect of the total witness asked of all followers of Jesus. So too the spirituality of John Paul II is essential for us, because *Totus Tuus,* the total giving of self, does not end at Nazareth, it is consummated at Calvary. All of us as a *Totus Tuus* people must be willing to courageously carry our crosses unto Calvary. Furthermore, we must keep before the eyes of our heart the certainty that if we follow Our Lady to Calvary, then we will also follow her to the Resurrection and to Pentecost, for she is the first and pre-eminent Disciple of the Lord Jesus.

What could prevent us from joining our Mother Coredemptrix at Calvary? What could keep us from answering the call of St. Paul to "make up what is lacking in the sufferings of Christ for the sake of His body, which is the Church" (Col. 1:24)? This passage from St. Paul is one of the most mysterious of all Scripture, one which, if we do not have an understanding of the Mystical Body, can appear to be blasphemy, assuming that we as mere creatures could "make up what is lacking" in the suffering of our God-Savior. With an understanding of the Mystical Body, however, we enter into a deeper awareness of what it means to be co-redeemers with Jesus our Redeemer, and with our Mother Coredemptrix.

What could prevent us from living more fully in this mystery? There are many factors, but foremost among them is the great spiritual obstacle of pride. It is pride that says we do not need a redeemer. There was a prevailing attitude in the 1970's in various sections of the West, which was captured in the expression, *"I'm OK, You're OK."* The presupposition of the attitude was that there is fundamentally no need to fear or worry about sin and Redemption from sin because there really is no original sin. In response, St. Augustine would have said, "I'm not OK, and you're not OK, but it's OK because of Christ!" We are able to face our fallen condition because we have been redeemed by a God who loves us even in our sin and weakness. But pride would have us deny the truth about ourselves; it would have us deny what the Holy Father calls, "the whole truth about man." Pride enters deeply into the heart, but also into the mind. How many have fallen to the great temptation of intellectual pride? Intellectual pride is a special difficulty for the educated, for those who hold office, for those who are called to speak and teach in the name of the Church. For those who are gifted intellectually, it is all too easy to succumb to the false notion that the head must dominate the heart, which can lead to an act of ecclesial disobedience based on one's own perceived "intellectual breakthrough," which can ultimately end in a position of theological dissent from authentic magisterial teachings. Instead, the mind must work in union with the heart—both suffused with grace—for in this way we are freed to make the act of loving obedience to the divine authority of Christ, as expressed through his Vicar on earth, and at the same time to use the mind for the glory of God, as captured in the classic definition of theology: *fides quarens intellectum* (faith seeking understanding).

Tragically, many in our own age have said, "I will decide what is true or not true; I will decide what I will obey; I will decide whether or not the Pope has discerned matters as astutely as I have." Such thinking opens the mind and heart to grave spiritual dangers. And when this attitude applies itself to the role of the Mother of God, we should not be surprised when it expresses itself in opinions such as, "I do not need to climb into the arms of my Mother, I can run myself."

Those of us who have the vocation of family life, of living in the *ecclesia domestica*, sometimes see examples of this in our children. Often a mother will be in a hurry, and will make the request to her three year old child, "Please, let me carry you. We're late. We must go quickly." And the child responds with obstinance, "No, mommy, I'll do it myself. I'll run." But the mother says, "Please, we're late. We must go quickly." And the child stubbornly says again, "No, I will run." But the willfulness and independence of the child delays greatly the work of the mother, for the full speed of the child's run is incomparable to the speed of the

Mother's run. We have the same invitation. Our Mother Coredemptrix is saying to each one of us, "Let me pick you up so we can run to our Eucharistic Jesus and to the Triumph of the Immaculate Heart, at a speed which you cannot obtain on your own."

We must learn to recognize within ourselves the voice which says, "No, mother, I'll run on my own." We must not listen to this voice. Instead, let us allow our Mother to pick us up and carry us to the Triumph. Let us have the humility of a child, as in the great spirituality of Saint Thérèse of Lisieux, the Little Flower, so that we can spiritually see that we are called to go to the breast of our Mother, Mediatrix of all grace, for the spiritual milk of sanctifying grace. It takes humility to accept that we do not know all the answers, to realize that we need the Mother. She is the Seat of Wisdom, and with her help we will retain the gifts of the intellect, but in proper submission to and unity with the divine presence in the heart of the soul, and in obedient submission to the Holy Father who himself, by the power of the Spirit, is in submission to the will of the Sacred and Immaculate Hearts of Jesus and Mary.

A second great obstacle to joining our Mother Coredemptrix at the foot of the cross is lack of perseverance. And here we are all called to examine our hearts, to examine our consciences. In our lives, have we had the experience of a great grace given to us by the Blessed Mother, but have not properly cooperated with that grace? Have our hearts been touched by her during a particular visit to the Blessed Sacrament, after receiving Holy Communion, during a Rosary, during a visit to a Marian shrine, during a visit to a Marian apparition site on pilgrimage? Has that touch grown cold? Have we failed to incorporate that grace into our daily Christian living? Can we think back to a moment when our Mother, Mediatrix of all grace, has been especially generous, and how at that moment we embraced her Immaculate Heart, but since then we have let it go to some degree, lost in our busy lives and daily agendas?

Those moments of special blessing must be made present again in our hearts with a renewed love and appreciation for the graces our Mother has given us in the past. We must also assist others to make this same Marian examination of conscience. Our beloved pastors, who are charged with the shepherding of souls, have a special calling to this renewal. Because all actual grace is temporary, it must be incorporated into the quasi-permanent gift of sanctifying grace, the grace intended by God to remain in the human heart and to grow dynamically *ad finitum*. And this renewal of the heart can be assisted by the gift of memory. We are called to remember those moments in the past when our Mother has touched us with the tenderness of her maternal kiss, and to renew and return that grace into our lives today. Let us visit that Marian shrine or pilgrimage location daily in our hearts, and re-kindle that zeal for Christ and the Church that we once obtained there.

We are also called to be Marian evangelizers. To preach and to teach the love of Mary is a prerequisite of the Triumph, and for this we must obtain a new boldness of heart. For many of us, some of the greatest offenses we suffered as children were those sad incidents when someone made a derogatory comment about our mother. If they criticized us, or criticized the place where we lived, or criticized our race or creed, oftentimes we were able to handle it. But if they criticized our mother, that was the "last straw." This is the courage we must obtain for the bold, stouthearted, but always charitable defense and evangelization of the message of Mary Coredemptrix. She persevered unto Calvary for us, amidst criticism and mockery of all sorts. Can we not endure the same for her and the truth about her?

Let us reflect on the following spiritual meditation, as if, following the traditions of the 17th century spiritual work, *Imitation of Mary,* our Blessed Mother would have personally conveyed these words of consolation and peace to each one of us:

> "Come my children, come, pray with me. I am here at the foot of my Son's Cross. I am here praying with you in front of the Blessed Sacrament. I am with you when you walk through your valleys and when you rejoice.
>
> "So many have come to pray with me, to rejoice with me, to weep with me, but

then have left again, drifting away from prayer, from union with my Son. Some feel the separation when they wander too far away and they come running back to Him at the foot of His Cross where I wait for them also with open arms. Some, however, wander very far away and become lost and afraid, but are too proud to call out for help. My heart weeps for these; woe be to them. If you know lost ones like this, please tell them that it is not too late to call out, I will gladly guide them back to my Son, but if they refuse, then pray for them that they will not be lost forever in darkness. Please know that I wish always to lead you to my Son, to guide you through the darkness into the light.

"Pray, pray, pray with me, then you shall always be in union with my Son, and you will no longer be in danger of wandering from His most Precious Heart.

"Come, rest between the heartbeats of His Sacred Heart and my Immaculate Heart."

Consecration to the Immaculate Heart of Mary

The ultimate *fiat*, the ultimate "yes" to our Mother Coredemptrix, and the ultimate pre-condition for further participating in the Triumph, is consecration to the Immaculate Heart of Mary.

What is consecration? Consecration is a promise of love and a gift of self which gives all that we are and all that we do, without limitation, to the Immaculate Heart of Mary so that she can bring us most perfectly to the Sacred Heart of Jesus. Marian consecration leads to the great fruit of most perfectly fulfilling our baptismal promises to Jesus Christ.

Origen, for example, tells us that the Christian life is nothing more than being true to our baptismal promises. Of course we can seek to live our baptismal promises on our own—"No, Mommy, I'll do it myself!" On the other hand, we can attempt to live our baptismal promises with the full God-given power of the Mediatrix of all grace. Why would we choose the former, when our Crucified Lord, from the cross, has offered us the latter? Where is the loss in giving ourselves to the Mother of Jesus? The only reason we might hesitate is if we did not truly know the person to whom we were giving ourselves.

Do we sometimes treat our Mother as if she were a stranger at the front door? When there is a stranger at the front door, we tend to deal with him there, because we do not know him; we do not invite him into our home. But when a neighbor comes to the front door, we invite him in with hospitality and ask him to enter the living room. If it is a family member at the front door, we go even further, saying, "My house is your house."

What do we say to the Mother of Jesus? Are we afraid to let the Mother of Jesus into our homes? Are we afraid that if we let her in that she might steal something? That she might take some of the coins off the counter? That she might steal a precious object? There is nothing to fear from the Mother of God! We must not be afraid to *let her into our homes entirely.*

"Seeing his mother there with the disciple whom he loved, Jesus said to his mother, 'Woman, there is your son.' In turn he said to the disciple, 'There is your mother.' From that hour onward, the disciple took her into his home" (Jn 19:26-27).

Our Holy Father, referring to this passage in his Marian encyclical, *Redemptoris Mater*, tells us that "We are all called to imitate John, the beloved disciple" (cf. n. 39). Mary is given to John from the lips of the Crucified as Mother. And in obedient love, the beloved Disciple takes Mary into his own home.

The Greek translation is not 'into his home,' but 'into his own.' The emphasis in the latter is on possession, not geography. Our Holy Father also tells us that the ultimate home, the ultimate *own*, is the human heart. Thus, we are called to give the Mother of Jesus complete access, unconditional entry and welcome, into our human hearts, into our interior lives, into our spiritual lives. We are to say to her, "Mother, my heart is yours." And as our Blessed Mother showed us at Fatima, in the seventh apparition to Sister Lucia in the 1920's, we are called to spiritually take our hearts from our chests and offer these hearts to the Immaculate Heart of Mary. She did it first! She first took her heart, a heart surrounded by thorns, and

25

offered it to us. Can we not give the Mother the same gift? This unconditional giving of our hearts to the Immaculate Heart of Mary is Marian consecration.

We are celebrating this year the tenth anniversary of *Redemptoris Mater*, the great encyclical of our Holy Father on the Mother of the Redeemer. In this encyclical, he calls us to the spirituality of Saint Louis Marie Grignon de Montfort. *"Totus Tuus ego suum et omnia mea tua sunt, O Virgo benedicta,"* I am entirely yours, and all that I have is yours, O Blessed Virgin.

The first fruit of Marian consecration is always a Eucharistic fruit. The Mother will always say to us what she said at Cana, "Do whatever He tells you" (Jn 2:5). Just as Vatican II called us to appreciate the Eucharist as the font and summit of the Christian life, our Mother Coredemptrix will always direct our hearts to an ever-greater love of our Eucharistic Jesus as the summit of our spiritual life. Marian consecration leads to the living of a Eucharistic spirituality with a Marian clarity, not on our own, but with the focus of the Immaculate One. She will always lead our hearts to adore Jesus in the tabernacle of our Churches and the tabernacles of our hearts.

How do we make our hearts tabernacles for Jesus? We have tabernacles throughout the world where we can adore Him, but we are also called to make our hearts *interior* tabernacles. We can prepare our hearts to be interior tabernacles with the indwelling Jesus by following the ancient formula for conversion, to be followed with the great sacrament of Reconciliation where we meet our sweet and merciful Divine Physician.

First of all, we must ask Our Lord to remove from our hearts any willfulness, any agenda, any attachments to worldly possessions, reputation, pride of position, authority, or power. We must remember always that our Mother loves the *Anawim*, the blessed little ones. And if we want her to pick us up and advance us in the spiritual life, we must become "little ones."

So, here again, a challenging examination of conscience is asked of us. Is there any title, or position, or possession that keeps us from staying at the foot of the Cross with our Mother Coredemptrix? If there is, we must offer that to her. Whatever keeps us from the Eucharistic Heart of Jesus must be given to our Mother to be purged, to be detached, to be purified.

Secondly, we must welcome the Eucharistic Jesus into our hearts. Remember the theological distinction, *ex opere operato* and *ex opere operantis*, which means that the objective grace of the sacrament is present, but the degree of the reception is dependent on our spiritual predisposition, our spiritual preparation. As many of the mystics and saints have said (Saint Teresa of Avila, Blessed Elizabeth of the Trinity), if we are baptized and in the state of grace, Jesus and the Trinitarian life dwells in our souls. We are walking tabernacles, and the awe of this must always be preserved. We must always keep in mind that wherever we go we bring the Father, Son, and Holy Spirit with us. Even if difficulties come, even if in the future there arise obstacles to reception of the Holy Eucharist, or if access to our Eucharistic Jesus is denied us, or visits to the tabernacles where our Eucharistic Jesus await us are prevented, such physical impediments (already experienced in some regions of the world) cannot prevent us from continuing to adore Him in the tabernacles in the monstrances of our heart.

If our Mother Coredemptrix could speak to each one of us living today during this climax of the "Age of Mary", would she not say:

> "I have come as your Mother, heed my call. Lift up your eyes and see the suffering of my Son whose Heart is pierced by the many sins of the world, and offer me your heart. Consecrate yourselves to my Immaculate Heart and the Sacred Heart of my Son. We beg you, we plead with you, listen, pray, convert yourselves. My Spouse inflames your heart with the fires of his love. Be still and listen to His words when He speaks for and to your hearts. Watch with me and remember my Son's Passion. Watch as He suffered for all mankind, so that sins may be forgiven. Keep watch with Him in all the tabernacles of the world. Do not leave Him. Allow your hearts to become tabernacles for His most precious Love and Mercy."

The Triumph of the Immaculate Heart

We have often heard the expression "the Triumph of the Immaculate Heart," first given to us in prophesy by Our Lady of the Rosary at Fatima. But what precisely is the Triumph of the Immaculate Heart of Mary? The Triumph of the Immaculate Heart is the gathering together of human hearts abandoned to Jesus and consecrated to Mary, those who form a Marian family, a Marian remnant, a Marian army willing to do all they can to bring about the Reign of the Most Sacred Heart of Jesus, the Reign of the Eucharist, the Era of Peace prophesied at Fatima, the new springtime for the Church. For any army to be efficient, there must be unity, subordination, and a clear recognition of authority. The heavenly authority for this army is the Immaculate Heart of Mary, and the earthly authority is the Vicar of Christ, our Holy Father, Pope John Paul II. We must learn to listen and hear his voice, for he is the teacher and prophet given to us by God, through whom Jesus speaks. There must be no confusion about this point. There is one commander on earth, and that is the Vicar of Christ, the *Totus Tuus* Pope.

Therefore, as co-redeemers united with Our Lady Coredemptrix, we must pray for our Holy Father. We must suffer for the Holy Father. We are called to offer the Sacrifice of the Mass, our Eucharistic communions, our Rosary intentions for him. If we are tempted by intellectual pride into thinking that, "No, the first thing we must do is write deep theological tracts, or put on Marian conferences, start Marian newsletters, etc., then we have fallen into the error of putting our mind first and the Immaculate Heart second. Ours is a battle first and foremost of prayer and fasting, united with the Sacrifice of the Mass, and only as a fruit of this do we undertake the serious and important tasks of articulating, clarifying, and promulgating the sublime, mysterious theological truth about she who is Coredemptrix, Mediatrix, and Advocate. But we must always remember that our Marian mission is primarily a battle of the heart, of prayer, a decisive struggle undertaken by all those who are united with the Immaculate Heart.

The Dogma of Our Lady
Coredemptrix, Mediatrix, Advocate

What is the role of the solemn papal definition of Mary Coredemptrix, Mediatrix, and Advocate in the Triumph of the Immaculate Heart? The solemn declaration of this dogma by the Vicar of Christ initiates, in a profound way, the Triumph of our Blessed Mother. It is the key that unlocks the graces of the Triumph, that ushers in superabundant graces for the Triumph of the Immaculate Heart. It also opens the floodgates of unique graces, allowing her to intercede with the fullest possible mediation given to her by God for this Triumph, for the Church and for humanity.

Let us recall that decisive moment on March 25, 1984, when the Pope consecrated the world to the Immaculate Heart of Mary. And let us be very clear about its full significance. Despite many doubts and criticisms, the consecration was accomplished by our Holy Father and accepted by Heaven. This was confirmed both by Sr. Lucia of Fatima and by the Holy Father. In these times we must beware of confusion and distraction that can come from many quarters. We must never lose sight of the true components of the Triumph. The consecration of the world, inclusive of Russia, to the Immaculate Heart was completed. Why was it so important? Because it allowed our Blessed Mother to intercede in a powerful way. She respects our freedom just as God the Father respects our freedom. Love never forces itself upon us; Heaven waits for us to ask. In this sense, our Heavenly Mother is limited by our freedom in exercising her full God-given power of mediation. We must freely acknowledge her as Coredemptrix, Mediatrix, and Advocate so that she can fully exercise these roles for us at this watershed of human history. And thus, much depends on us. An integral part of the grace of the Triumph is the precondition of the Church requesting that it come.

Therefore, the solemn declaration of Our Lady Coredemptrix, Mediatrix, and Advocate as Dogma by the Vicar of Christ ushers in, in a way both profound and supernatural, the Triumph of the Immaculate Heart. It is the key that unlocks the inestimable graces of the Triumph.

Her titles are her works, her titles are her functions, and the solemn proclamation of our Mother's titles will lead to the full release of her most powerful sanctifying functions of grace and peace for the many crises experienced in the contemporary Church and world.

Among these graces will be the grace necessary for an authentic Christian unity. Too long have we thought that one new theological insight would bring us into union with our Orthodox brothers and sisters, and with our other non-Catholic brothers and sisters. But insights alone will accomplish little in this regard. Above all we need the supernatural help of the Mother. Union will come through the unifying of our hearts in our common love for the Mother of God. The union of our hearts in the Heart of the Mother of God will be the supernatural means of union of the Churches of the East and West. When we humbly acknowledge that we do indeed need the help of the Mother of God for authentic Christian unity, we will have the beginnings of ultimate Christian union in the one Body of Christ. The role of this papal definition is pivotal. We must pray with the fullness of our hearts for this definition, and use all the resources of our minds for its accomplishment.

There must be a full Marian family effort to bring forth this great dogmatic fruit, this historic fruit for the Church and for the world. Let us do all that we can to bring about the prophetic words of our Blessed Mother which would be climaxed in this great Marian Dogma: "All generations shall call me blessed."

Prayer

Sweet Mother Coredemptrix, we confess our great unworthiness to be your instruments leading to the Triumph of your Immaculate Heart. But we remember the words of Saint Gabriel, the Archangel, spoken to you at the very moment of the Annunciation, that "with God, all things are possible."

With that trust, not in ourselves, but in you, we offer ourselves afresh to the cause of the Triumph, in complete obedience to our beloved Holy Father, Pope John Paul II. Use us, we pray, as Marian apostles, spreading the truth about your role in salvation history, about your titles and roles as our Coredemptrix, Mediatrix of all grace, and Advocate, to the four corners of the earth. We ask the holy angels to lead us to be authentic missionaries of your Immaculate Heart. Remembering our unworthiness, Mother, we ask for your grace, which strengthens and sustains us like nothing else, leading us to be true to our Eucharistic Jesus, and ultimately to our Abba, Father, from whom all things come, through the sanctifying power of the Holy Spirit.

Hail Mary, full of grace, the Lord is with thee. Blessed art thou among women, and blessed is the fruit of thy womb, Jesus. Holy Mary, Mother of God, pray for us sinners now and at the hour of our death. Amen.

St. Joseph, Patron of the Church, pray for us. Amen.

The Dogma and the Triumph

Chapter 2

Our Lady Coredemptrix and our Eucharistic Jesus

"O Come Let Us Adore Him"

What are the foundations of a Marian dogma? Why would a new Marian dogma be so interconnected with our Eucharistic Jesus and the critical necessity for an international renewal of Eucharistic adoration?

The *Vox Populi Mariae Mediatrici* movement is based on the three pillars that historically led to the Dogma of the Immaculate Conception proclaimed by Pius IX in 1854, and the Dogma of the Assumption, proclaimed by Pius XII in 1950. These three critical elements are: 1) the theological foundations, 2) the response of the hierarchy, and 3) the response of the *sensus fidelium*, the common consensus of the faithful. Let us reflect on each of these pillars.

1) The appropriate theological foundations for the declaration of the Dogma of Mary as Coredemptrix, Mediatrix and Advocate are considerable. Numerous papal teachings and some of the most esteemed theo-

logians in the world have confirmed that the revealed truth of Mary Coredemptrix, Mediatrix, Advocate is already clearly doctrinally present in Sacred Scripture, in Apostolic Tradition, and in the nineteenth and twentieth century teachings of the Papal Magisterium. It is present in the Magisterium of the Church in a special way in the teachings of our present Holy Father, Pope John Paul II.

The question could be asked, "Why do we need a definition, if this truth is already Magisterial teaching?" Pius IX answered that question at the time he defined the Dogma of the Immaculate Conception. He taught that a dogma is the *perfection* of a doctrine. The Church never creates doctrine. In a dogmatic declaration the Church exercises its greatest, most specific articulation of the truth in order to bring to fruition the fullest possible appreciation of that truth in the life of the faithful, and to open wide the doors to tremendous graces for the Church and the world.

2) The response of the hierarchy has been outstanding. Recently, our Holy Father, Pope John Paul II, was presented with over 500 Episcopal endorsements of the dogma from Cardinals and Bishops worldwide, letters gathered within the last three and one half years. This figure does not include the Episcopal endorsements in great numbers which have been sent to the Popes since the 1920's, but includes only those successors of the Apostles of today. Clearly, there has been a tremendous manifestation of hierarchical support in the recent years.

3) The response of the *sensus fidelium*, the common consensus of the faithful. The papal documents, *Ineffabilis Deus*, in 1854, which defined the Dogma of the Immaculate Conception, and *Munificentissimus Deus*, in 1950, which defined the Dogma of the Assumption, both refer to the millions of petitions from the faithful which encouraged the definition of these Dogmas. We must remember the ancient Church axiom, "Vox populi, vox Dei," the voice of the people is the voice of God.

The Popes have always been very sensitive to the voice of the people, and have at certain periods in the history of the Church relied upon this voice to preserve orthodoxy. For example, during our greatest doctrinal crisis, the Arian heresy of the 4th century, a large number of the members of the hierarchy, due to various political, theological and spiritual pressures, abandoned orthodox doctrine, even to the point of denying the divinity of Jesus Christ. During that terrible time when, as Saint Jerome says, "the whole world awoke to find itself Arian," the Pope and the lay faithful remained true to the Catholic faith. Hence, the subsequent popes have maintained a perennial respect for the *sensus fidelium*.

During the past three and one half years the *Vox Populi* of our times, in a remarkable manifestation of the *sensus fidelium*, has gathered approximately 4.6 million petitions from 157 countries for the papal definition of Our Lady Coredemptrix, Mediatrix, Advocate. For the Dogma of the Assumption, the average number of petitions was one hundred thousand per year. The average number of petitions for the dogma of the Maternal Mediation of our Lady Coredemptrix has been one million petitions per year.

Thus, we can be confident that in requesting this definition we stand on the most solid ecclesial ground. Yet, beyond these three elements we must also remember the essential role of the spiritual life of *Vox Populi Mariae Mediatrici* and all hearts consecrated to the Immaculate Heart is prayer, and in a special way, Eucharistic prayer.

Prayer is the requirement for all true movements in the Church, and in this must be included the myriad of different forms of prayer, including sacrifices, visible and invisible. Many hidden souls are involved in this work, people who continue to offer much suffering, penance, and fasting; those who have been called to become the contemplative members, and those who are undergoing great trials, as the "victim" members of *Vox Populi* who offer all their merits for the declaration of the dogma. Through the spiritual and active labors of all members of the Marian family, we have arrived on the threshold of a great historic moment.

Modeling ourselves upon our Blessed Mother, we know that central to all these spiritual labors is our love for the Eucharist. For a true Marian apostle is ultimately a Eucharistic apostle. As the first fruit of our Marian consecration, Our Mother Coredemptrix leads us always and in every way to her Eucharistic Son. We must never forget that it was the Virgin of

Nazareth, who through her free cooperation, first gave the world the Body and Blood of Jesus Christ. It was she who gave flesh to the Word conceived in her womb by the power of the Holy Spirit. Therefore, whenever we receive the Eucharist, the real Body, Blood, Soul, and Divinity of Our Lord Jesus Christ, we should always have the intention of thanking the Mother who made the Eucharist possible by first giving Jesus His perfect human nature, which we receive in the Eucharist in its resurrected and glorified form.

Preparation for Receiving our Eucharistic Jesus

In chapter 6 of Saint John's Gospel, often called the "Eucharistic Chapter," Jesus tells us:

> "I am the bread of life ... Truly, truly, I say to you, unless you eat the flesh of the Son of man, and drink His blood, you have no life in you; he who eats My flesh and drinks My blood has eternal life, and I will raise him up on the last day. For My flesh is food indeed, and My blood is drink indeed. He who eats My flesh and drinks My blood abides in Me, and I in him" (Jn 6:48, 53ff).

Bread remains the staple of human existence throughout the world. So too the Eucharist is the nourishment for our spiritual life, the "Bread come down from Heaven" (Jn 6:33). Let us never lose sight of our *greatest spiritual sustenance,* which Jesus offers us daily in the Eucharistic miracle. The old translation of the *Pater Noster* in the Vulgate conveys this truth emphatically: "*Panum nostrum superstantialem da nobis hodie.*" "Give us this day our supersubstantial bread," a bread that is more than material bread, but is the Body, Blood, Soul and Divinity of God Himself.

How many of us, if we had the opportunity to meet with John Paul II for twenty minutes every day, would miss the opportunity? And yet we have a greater call — to meet the Eucharistic Lord every day, and not only to meet Him, but to *receive* Him into ourselves, into our own hearts. The primary intention of our heart, therefore, must be to place Him first in our lives. This means we have to sacrifice some of our many pressing duties and change our daily schedules if they interfere with this great gift. We must place our hearts on the surgeon's table, and we must let our Mother do any type of heart surgery necessary, so that we realize that our first call each day is the Eucharistic call. And if radical heart surgery is what is necessary, let us trust our Mother to do it. Whatever it takes in a change of heart or change of schedule, leading to the clear prioritizing of our day as the reception of our Eucharistic Jesus at daily Mass is that to which Marian apostles are called.

Let us ask ourselves if our thinking has become based on a wrong hierarchy of values. Have we ever gone through a day when we received Our Lord's Body and Blood at Mass, but at the end of the day we said, "Today was an unproductive day. I didn't accomplish anything. Today was a wasted day." Yet the truth of the matter is, if we have received God in the Eucharist the day has been a day of grace. If our hearts have become cluttered and anxious with many concerns, if we are haunted by a sense that there is not enough time to accomplish our tasks, then some radical surgery is needed. We must again ask our Mother to do any type of operation necessary to restore us to a spiritual priority of values and to the primacy of the Eucharist in our lives. If we need a bypass, if we need a quadruple bypass, if we need a transplant, she can do it.

The Eucharist must be our first love. It is not simply an added grace, it is the necessary grace. The Eucharist is the food on which our souls depend for life. It is also our spiritual refuge and protection. Our beloved priests are especially in need of this grace. Those blessed souls who have been given the great privilege of offering the Sacrifice of the Mass must see their primary role as the *alter Christus*, the "other Christ," uniting themselves to the sacrifice of Calvary through the Sacrifice of the Holy Mass. They must say to themselves: "This is what I am called to be. I am a priest in the order of Melchizedek. And my first responsibility is to offer the Sacrifice for God's people. This is what defines me. If I do nothing else, if I do no writing, if I do not meet with councils, even if I do not tend to the business and administration, still I have done my priestly task, for I have offered the eternal Sacrifice."

We faithful must revere the priesthood. We should be in awe by what it means to have the power to make God present. We are dependent on priests, for they bring us the gift that is more valuable than life itself. And we must let them know how grateful we are, how much we love them for sacrificing their lives so that we might have the Food that leads to eternal life.

Sadly, we must beware of a very dangerous tendency that is growing within theological circles and has become widespread in the Western world. This is a type of erroneous theology which would reduce the Sacrifice of the Mass to a meal. We must always respect the primacy of the sacrifice of Calvary which provides this Eucharistic food for us. The altar is first of all the altar of Sacrifice and then, as a result of the sacrifice, the table of the Eucharistic meal. We must beware of any undermining of the primacy of the Sacrifice, especially any implicit and explicit denials of the Sacrifice in liturgical practice. Not only does this radically oppose classic dogmatic theology, but in the words of the late Hans Urs von Balthasar, it leaves us prone to "celebrating ourselves first, and Christ second."

If the Mass becomes a "horizontal" celebration, focusing mainly on you-with-me and I-with-you, the sacrifice of Jesus and its vertical reconciliation in justice and mercy with the Eternal Father is pushed aside, and becomes only an afterthought. This can be a sort of human idolatry. We must always remember that the

Catholic Faith is both immanent *and* transcendent, horizontal *and* vertical, forming the arms of a Cross, embracing the whole world but drawing its life from Heaven. Heresy has been roughly defined as "mistaking the part for the whole." And so any attempt to reduce the content of our faith to a single part will lead to increasing spiritual blindness, distorted beliefs, and the sins which lead to spiritual death.

There is a grave warning for us in the book of Daniel 11:31, where the prophet refers to the great sacrilege by the enemy of God who removes the sacrifice from the temple: "Forces from him shall appear and profane the temple and fortress, and shall take away the continual burnt offering. And they shall set up the abomination that makes desolate" (Revised Standard Version, Catholic edition). Another translation renders this passage as follows: "Armed forces shall move at his command and defile the sanctuary stronghold, abolishing the daily sacrifice and setting up the horrible abomination." (New American Bible), and alternatively, "He shall take away the continual sacrifice, and they shall place there the abomination unto desolation" (Douay-Rheims Version). To celebrate ourselves instead of Christ at Calvary is an abomination. But in right order, with the sacrifice of Calvary we must partake of the Meal, for we need the Meal to continue to be about the labors and love at the service of the Sacred and Immaculate Hearts of Jesus and Mary.

Liturgically, if we place the sacrifice second to the meal, we are treading dangerously close to the offense which Daniel describes, for is it not an abomination to seek to pull God down from the throne of his divinity and to exalt man in his place? Grievously, there is much evidence of this in the western world. It is a creeping spiritual cancer, one which often grows quietly, without alerting many of the faithful to the real significance of what is happening. As any physician knows, the first step in restoration to health is identification of the cancer. Next, the cancer must be removed before it causes death to the entire body. Let us ask ourselves if there is indeed a cancer which seeks to exalt man over God within the Church or within the Liturgy, or which seeks to reduce the most important event in the history of the world to a matter of secondary importance.

Consider how in many churches the corpus has been removed from the cross? And yet it is a timeless truth of our faith that we cannot glory in the Resurrection unless we first share in the Passion. The crucifixion of our Lord is not merely an historical incident, completed, over with forever. Remember what Saint Paul says in Colossians 1:24: "...and in my flesh I complete what is lacking in the sufferings of Christ, for the sake of His Body, which is the Church." Christ's Redemption was accomplished fully on Calvary, but in His great love for us, because His heart's desire is for us to share in his glory, He has given us the gift of participating in His Cross. So if we are ever called to any degree of ecclesial passion and death, we have the example of our Lord Jesus, not only in soul but in incarnate body who could say to us, "I took the wounds first. That is why you can follow me."

As the old maxim states, "No Cross, No Crown." Removal of the corpus from the cross implies that, "we are fully Resurrected already." A common sense of reality alone should tell us that we are a pilgrim Church, we have not yet arrived in the glory of Heaven. That is why we need the example of the crucified Christ, so that we are reminded to draw our life from His sacrifice daily in the Mass. If a time should come when we experience persecution, mockery, scourging, or some form of crucifixion spiritually or bodily for the name of Christ and the fullness of the Church, we will have before the eyes of our hearts the powerful image of Jesus on the Cross, the Crucified One who did it all before us and for us.

In some churches in the West, kneelers are being removed. Although there is a tradition in the Eastern Catholic rites of not using kneelers, it is important to note that Byzantine Catholics have a powerful spirituality of *proskynousi*, or profound veneration throughout the sacred liturgy of the Eucharist. In Lenten liturgies there is a tradition of prostrating the whole body before the Lord in great humility and a spirit of repentance. The Eastern rites are saturated in a spirit of deep reverence, a strong sense of the transcendent, and a developed awareness of the glory of God. These spiritual senses are declining in the West, which is all the more reason why our relatively minor gestures of reverence ought not be taken away. The real question is what is *the intention*, what is the motivation, behind the move to eliminate kneelers? Is it not a symptom of growing hesitancy to *genu flectatur*, to bend the knee in the presence of the Divine? If the angels fall in prostration in the presence of the Divine, should *we* refuse to bend the knee? Are the Catholic people of the West becoming too proud to be in a position of submission, bodily reverence, and humility when the Sacrifice of Christ is being offered? A flawed theology is perhaps at the root of this problem, the erroneous belief that we can enhance our dignity by reducing our humility before God. This is a tragically stunted viewpoint, for the truth is we find our ultimate dignity in Jesus Himself who first made the historic kenosis, He who first humbled himself, obedient unto death, even unto death on a cross (cf. Phil 2:5-11).

The most alarming symptom of this spiritual cancer is the removal of the Eucharistic presence from some of our churches. There are parishes that have not only removed the Eucharistic presence from the sanctuary, but have removed it altogether from the church. Church teaching permits, in certain circumstances, a Blessed Sacrament chapel to be used for reservation of the Sacrament. But such teaching was never intended to become the norm in ordinary parishes to remove the Eucharistic presence from the main chapels.

There are other disturbing liturgical and architectural developments. For example, in some newly constructed churches one finds that the altar has been placed to the left of the sanctuary, and the central position is now occupied by the "presider's chair." What is being said liturgically here? What is being said about the primacy of Jesus Christ, and about the *presence* of Jesus. How is this forming our children? Who and what are we celebrating? Have we lost the spirit of "Zeal for thy house consumes me?" (cf. Jn 2:17, Ps 69:10). When our Eucharistic Jesus is systematically removed from churches, or when in some degree He is reduced in importance and delegated to less significant locations in our churches, we sadly must admit that at that point we no longer have churches which are fully houses of the Father dedicated to the Son.

Much of the cancer has spread under the banner of "building community." It bears repeating here that this is an important aspect of our faith-life, but it will fail unless it is firmly grounded in the Eucharist. The Eucharist is the source of any authentic community. The Eucharist is the source of Jesus within each other. We are united not only with Jesus in the Sacrament, but with other members of the Mystical Body of Christ. When we receive His Body and Blood He "abides in us," and we "abide in Him" by entering more profoundly into his Mystical Body which is the Church. As a true Eucharistic and Marian remnant, ours is ultimately a Eucharistic *union of hearts* nourished by the Body and Blood of the Lord, a union which does not end at the conclusion of Mass. For as

He "abides in us" and we "abide in Him" we return to our homes or workplaces bearing Him in the interior tabernacles, in the "heart of the soul." If we want our collective hearts to act as one unified heart in complete union with the Immaculate Heart of Mary, we must be centered on the Eucharist, and the power of the Eucharist.

How, then, should we properly prepare to receive this great gift? First of all we must renew our awareness that Jesus is giving Himself entirely to us. But how can bread and wine become God, we may wonder? How can the Infinite place Himself in a mode in which finite creatures can receive Him? Metaphysically, and theologically, and ontologically, how can He do it? Only by becoming humble will we begin to understand the humility of God. He first empties Himself. He becomes man through the womb of the Virgin Mary, a creature who gives birth to a Creator. Then He becomes sacrament, so that we—frail, human, limited vessels—can receive the infinite. We too are called to be like Mary, for God in His infinite love for us desires to dwell within us, desires that we become living tabernacles.

In order to prepare ourselves for this indwelling, we must be in the state of sanctifying grace. Thus, we should have frequent recourse to the Sacrament of Confession. In a world without sin we would have no need for confession. But each of us is marked by the effects of original sin, and we fall to actual sin, and for this reason we should strive to meet the Divine Physician as often as possible. Making a practice of regular confession not only strengthens us to avoid the danger of mortal sin, but it also purifies the tabernacles of our hearts. Why have so many people developed a negative understanding of the Sacrament of Reconciliation? Some of it is due to ignorance and poor catechesis; some of it is due to embarrassment and fear of what the priest might think of us. But this is to forget that the Lord loves us even in the midst of our sinfulness. He loves us with perfect knowledge of the "whole truth about man." Why would we ever hesitate to come trustingly before this love? Why would we be afraid to expose our darkness to this wonderful light? When we enter the confessional with our sins and proper contrition of the heart, we are freed from our sins through the power of the priest; we are given sacramental grace to avoid the sins we are prone to commit, and we have met Christ who wishes to heal our souls.

Many of our beloved pastors and priests are generous in giving the faithful the opportunity to cleanse our souls. Yet, in their desire to be available to us, many pastors do not seek *for themselves* this very same grace, forgetting that priests too need to be purified and strengthened so that they can be ever greater ministers of the Church and its sacraments. Our beloved priests need the spiritual fortification of frequent confession, perhaps more now than ever before, to continue to be on the front lines of the great battle between the Woman and the serpent.

It takes humility of the heart to confess one's sins to another human being. What does humility of the heart mean? Humility comes from the word *humus*—earth, ground, the soil from which we were created. It takes humility to realize that without God we are nothing. With God, we can be anything He chooses us to be. St. Augustine says, "We need three virtues for growth in the spiritual life: humility, humility, and humility." The foundation of humility is realizing that God is the source of life. We are so dependent on Him that we cannot even respond to His grace without Him first giving us the grace to receive it. St. Augustine tells us, "You need grace to merit grace." In other words, we need actual grace to receive sanctifying grace.

Allow me to use an example from the domestic Church: Let us say it is a Friday, a few days before Father's Day, and a seven year old child comes up to his father and says, "Father, I would like to give you a gift for Father's Day, but I have no money. Could you give me a few dollars?"

"Yes, son," the Father replies, smiling.

"Father, I have no way to get down to the store. Could you bring me?"

"Yes, son."

"Father, I would like to get you a tie, but I don't know which one. Could you choose one?"

"Yes, son."

"Father, I want to wrap your present, but I don't know how. Could you buy the paper and show me?"

"Yes, son."

"And, Father, I want to wrap it with a ribbon, but I don't know which one or how to put the ribbon on."

"Yes, son."

The morning of Father's Day arrives and the child brings the father his gift. A tear runs down the father's cheek in thanksgiving and gratitude. Someone might ask him, "What are you crying about? You chose the gift, you bought the gift, you wrapped it—why the sentimentality?"

The father replies: "Because it was the *intention of the heart of my child* to give this to me. And even though I did everything else, his intention touches my heart."

This is what the Eternal Father, the "Abba" says to us: "I give you the grace, I give you every actual grace necessary to help at every step. Then I give you the sanctifying grace to perform and sustain your good work. I need the freely given intention of your heart and that is all." A saint is a person who has chosen in his heart to simply cooperate fully with the grace given by the Father. And that is what we too are called to do. But it takes humility of heart, like the little child going to his father, asking for all that he needs.

The late Mother Teresa tells us, "The task of sanctity is simply not getting in the way of God's design. We are nothing more than the pencils in the hand of the Father." We of the Marian remnant are little pencils, and sometimes we feel that we are broken or worn down pencils. But our Mother can still use us if we have the intention to cooperate. Indeed, she wishes to use us because we *are* small and weak. Humility of the heart knows that all things are possible with God. And through his most perfect creature, the Woman, He is calling us to be evangelists of our Eucharistic Jesus. How could we keep this spiritual treasure to ourselves? Can we not hear our meek and merciful Jesus speaking to our hearts, especially when we pray in His Eucharistic presence:

> "Silence, My child. Silence all within you, so you can hear My voice whispering to you in the silence of your soul. I wish to speak to you about My Love and Mercy which waits for all My children in the silence of all the tabernacles throughout the world.
>
> "Come to Me when your heart is burdened or your heart is light, come to Me in all the stages of your life. Do not be afraid to come to Me for I am your Merciful Savior who wishes to extend My Mercy to all those who come to Me with a sorrowful and repentant heart.
>
> "Do not be too proud to come to Me, for your pride will cause you great harm and will separate you from Me.
>
> "Humility shall bring you closest to Me, for it is a humble heart that receives Me most completely, and a humble heart

that I fill to its greatest capacity with My Love and Mercy.

"A humble heart has no bounds, no constrictions to prevent it from being stretched and molded to receive a never-ending flow of My Love.

"A humble heart does not fear My Will but clings to My ways, knowing that I Will only the best for My children.

"A humble heart does not flee from Me in times of distress, temptation, or failure, but flies unto the refuge and shelter of My Heart of Love and Mercy, and solicits My help and guidance to lead it through the storms and trials of this world.

"A humble heart does not scorn or cause others to stumble and fall, but it is a generous heart wishing to share all the riches of My Love and Mercy with all those whom they encounter in their lives.

"A humble heart shows My Love and Mercy to all, for they are filled with My Spirit, and none other. Their breath is My own, their heartbeat My own, their reflection My own.

"Come to Me, My children, with a humble and contrite heart and I shall give you life, true life, and I shall give you love, true love that will last forever, not just a lifetime, but for all eternity.

"Come unto Me like little children, and
I will set you free."

The Ecclesial Cry for Eucharistic Adoration

Our Lady Coredemptrix calls us to the Eucharistic Sacrifice and Banquet each day. She also calls each of us to her side where she is also present in a real sense with her Eucharistic Son. With her are the angels, in perpetual adoration of God. So often we go through our day-to-day life amidst the distractions of the human civilization completely unaware that there is a higher created civilization, populated by the great choirs of angels. We must also seek to conform our hearts to the angelic heart.

During the apparitions of the Angel of Peace at Fatima in 1916, the angel instructed the three young visionaries how they should pray in adoration and reparation for sins against the Eucharist. "O my God, I believe, I adore, I trust, and I love Thee. I beg pardon for those who do not believe, do not adore, do not trust, and do not love Thee." As the Angel of Peace instructed the children of Fatima, should we not also pray in this fashion as spiritual children of the same Mother?

We must imitate the angels in Eucharistic adoration, for our primary calling as creatures is to love and adore our Creator. But God also desires this because adoration of the Eucharist is the greatest remedy for the troubles of our day, especially when united with the Rosary. In that unified prayer, we have the Sacred Eucharistic Heart of Jesus and the Immaculate Heart of Mary pleading together the ultimate petition to the Abba, Father for the People of God.

I would like to offer you a symbol of the battle in which we are involved. Of course, we should not be preoccupied with the sense of battle to the extent that we lose sight of the fact that the ultimate victory has been assured. Our Mother has told us that her Immaculate Heart will triumph. She did not say the victory was conditional. It will surely happen. But we must remember that, to the extent that we do not respond to her requests, many, many souls will be lost.

In this battle, I want to give you symbolic images for the two opposing sides. The nature of the first side can be seen in that tragic historical event, the French revolution. During the reign of terror, men without faith sought to reject God and the authority of God, and seemed to win a temporary victory. At the height of the depravity and bloodshed the revolutionaries erected an altar to the goddess Reason: "Reason is our God!" This is human idolatry in its most belligerent form. Here we see a foreshadowing of the materialism of atheistic communism. The communist philosophy tells us in the words of Marx, quoting Schellmacher, "Philosophers have explained the world. Now it is time to change the world." These philosophers said, "There is no God. Therefore, if we want to change the world, we must do it ourselves."

The fruit of this ideology was seen within a few

short years when Josef Stalin destroyed an estimated 30 million of his own Russian people during the Great Purge. In seeking to usurp the authority of God by exalting man's power, he brought about untold suffering and destruction for man.

Similarly, Freemasonry leads its devotees to the idolatry of man under the guise of belief in God. Its most heinous ingredient is *compromise*, the incremental destruction of truth, beauty, goodness, and faith. It says, "Authority is evil, and the greatest evil is the authority represented in the Pope." In its founding days, Masonry focused attention directly against the authority of the Holy Father. And in our century this attack has not ceased, though it has become more subtle in some aspects. Maximilian Kolbe, when he was a young seminarian in Rome, once witnessed a Masonic demonstration in Saint Peter's Square, in which Masons paraded with a banner depicting the devil destroying the Archangel Michael, and chanting abuses against the Pope and his authority. The virulent hatred for the Church expressed by this group of demonstrators alerted Maximilian to the dangers of the times, and led him to form the Knights of the Immaculata as a Marian group to battle Masonry. He knew that when man is idolized, when reason is enthroned, one of the first victims of the revolution against God is reason itself.

Do we not see in our own generation a certain homage to the goddess of Reason? The most frightening technological powers ever developed in human history have arisen in our times, powers over life and death that rightly belong to God alone: *in vitro* fertilization, embryonic freezing and experimentation, sperm banks; and now we are even on the brink of human cloning efforts. These frightening technological "developments" are saying to the Eternal Father, "We do not need you, God. We can create ourselves." And with the advent of the nuclear age we now have the power to destroy the entire planet, which is saying to the Father, "If *we* decide to, we can destroy ourselves and everything You have made on this earth." Man has used his God-given powers of reason without submission to God's laws, and therefore, as in the French revolution, one of the first victims is reason itself.

The second image of the two opposing sides of the present battle is that of Our Blessed Mother, who is the absolute antithesis to the idolatrous altar of reason. Where do we find her? We find her before the altar of the one true God, adoring the Eucharistic Jesus in the Blessed Sacrament. In contrast to the noise and bloodshed of revolution, we find loving silence and mercy. The silence of this adoration cries out to heaven more powerfully than all the clamor around the altar of the goddess Reason. As we pray with Mary before our Eucharistic Jesus, we are saying, "Man is not first; God is first. Reason is not first, humility is first. Doing is not first, being is first - and the sanctification of being." The idolatry of reason is man so proud that he thinks that he is God; the Eucharist is God so humble that He became man, and emptied Himself once more to become Sacrament.

We are images of the Divine. We were created in the image and likeness of God, and thus we will not be happy until we are restored to union with him. Our Eucharistic Jesus exposed in the monstrance cries out silently for us to return to Him, to submit our reason to God's revelation. Adoration of the Blessed Sacrament is the greatest response a human being can make to God's love poured out over the world. We must not be drawn into the clamor of the altar of the goddess Reason; instead we must go in silence to the altar of the one true God, uniting ourselves with the untold legions of holy angels and with our Blessed Mother, and there to adore with them our incarnate Savior-God. Our Mother, in the silence of her Immaculate Heart, teaches us to worship "in spirit and in truth." Her triumphant Heart will lead us to Jesus' triumphant Eucharistic Heart.

What draws us to adoration? Humility of heart. The humility that says, "I need God. I am a creature and He is my Creator. I am not primary, I do not have to be in charge, I do not even have to use my creative, liturgical talents to make this adoration a 'success'." Our task is simply to be docile, to receive, to respond, to come before Him, to rest in the radiant silence of His presence. He will do the rest. He will sanctify us. This is the most powerful force in the world, but it is gentle and usually hidden from our own senses. Even so, in adoration we are radiated with His love and grace, just as on a day when the sky is overcast, and you find to your surprise at the end of the day that you have been slightly sunburned. When we are in the presence of the Divine, we can be burned, but this is not a sun or a fire that destroys; it is a Son and a Fire that gives life. Our hearts become inflamed with love of the Eucharist, love of Mary, and love of the Pope, a passion which does not come through the powers of human intellect, but through the heart. When we receive the Eucharist, the Heart of Jesus enters our very flesh and touches our own hearts.

To go to our Eucharistic Jesus is like receiving a blood transfusion from the Sacred Heart Himself. In humility, we must see that all of us need such a blood transfusion. And the greater our task for the Church, the greater the need for our transfusion.

The Gospel of Mark recounts the following event in the life of Christ:

> "There was a woman in the area who had been afflicted with a hemorrhage for a dozen years... She had heard about Jesus and came up behind him in the crowd and put her hand to his cloak. 'If I just touch his clothing,' she thought, 'I shall get well.' Immediately her flow of blood dried up and the feeling that she was cured of her affliction ran through her whole body. Jesus was conscious at once that healing

power had gone out from him. Turning about in the crowd, he began to ask, 'Who touched me?' His disciples said to him, 'You can see how this crowd hems you in, yet you ask, "Who touched me?"' Despite this, he kept looking around to see the woman who had done it. Fearful and beginning to tremble now as she realized what had happened, the woman came and fell in front of him and told him the truth. He said to her, 'Daughter, it is your faith that has cured you. Go in peace and be free of this illness'" (Mk 5:25-34).

That is the power of Jesus, who by his very being and nature heals and sanctifies. What would prevent us from running to meet Him in Eucharistic adoration? What are the obstacles? Sadly there are a few, and foremost among them is once again the great spiritual obstacle of pride. Pride says, "I do not need a divine healer. I do not need adoration. I can do it myself. I can serve my function in the Church quite well without any help." We must beware of the evil one who wishes to delude us with such thoughts. Satan will inevitably tempt hearts consecrated to the Immaculate Mother, but he will not do so with temptations to murder, rape, and pillage. Rather, he will tempt us with "good things" and good acts that are lesser goods than that to which He truly calls us. He will subtly try to draw us away from the highest good.

He will attempt to scatter our energies by leading us into many worthwhile projects that are not, in fact, the work which God has specifically asked of us. He will use anything and everything to inject confusion and distraction into our thinking, and he may even use secondary works of the Church to draw us away from our first call to receive and to adore the Eucharist; he will try to distract us from the critical call for every human heart to humble himself in silent adoration of our Eucharistic God. But our Mother proclaims instead, "O come, let us adore Him."

All of us must maintain vigilance in this regard. In humility of heart we must recall often that Eucharistic reception *and Eucharistic adoration* is our highest duty, and our greatest need. Those in pastoral ministry have an especially urgent need for this spiritual strengthening, precisely because they are responsible for so many souls in the Mystical Body of Christ. The flock is thirsty. How can we bring the bucket of water to them if there is no water in the bucket? The greater our task for the Church, the greater is our need to be filled, so that we might feed and water the flock of God.

We could well imagine Our Eucharistic Lord, exposed for Adoration, saying to us:

> "My child, how My Heart cries for souls to come and rest with Me. So many souls are cold and weary, trapped in the pits of despair by their own free will

which keeps them separate from Me. Their pride, their fear, their lust for the world and its earthly treasures lure them away from Me, for these things cannot co-exist with humility of the heart, which is the greatest pathway to My Heart. The humble know that only I can provide them what they seek, and what they seek from Me is eternal, everlasting, imperish-able. I offer those who seek Me with hu-mility of the heart a covenant between their heart and Mine, that they shall be provided with My Love and Mercy, which shall guide and sustain their soul for all eternity.

"Tell My poor lost souls this: Tell them that their Eucharistic Jesus waits for them always. Help them to come to My Eucha-ristic Heart which burns with love for them."

We must pray to the Holy Spirit, the Divine Sanc-tifier, to give us a fresh understanding of the need for a "New Evangelization," and at the same time ask Him to help us see Eucharistic Adoration as its spiritual foundation, the greatest foundation for the Pope's call for the New Evangelization in the Third Millennium.

One common objection to Eucharistic Adoration is that "it focuses on private devotion, and fails to concern itself with the social needs of the Church and the New Evangelization." In response, let us recall that the Holy Father has repeatedly called the faithful to adoration of the Eucharist. Let us also learn from the wisdom of the Church and Saint Thérèse of Lisieux. The Little Flower was proclaimed by the Church as co-patroness (with Saint Francis Xavier) of missionary activity. At a superficial glance one might say, "What nonsense! She never left the Carmel! She never crossed the street! Why would you make her co-patroness of the missions?" Here the Church is teaching us something of utmost importance: We must never forget that the foundation of all apostolic endeavors, including all missionary activity and evangelization, is the hidden contemplative and Eucharistic soul, for the adoring soul draws down untold graces, gives spiritual food and life to the missionary in doing the active work of God. There are the Mary and the Martha, both of whom are necessary for the Mystical Body.

We can recall the historic moment in the Philippines, when the unjust Marcos dictatorship threatened to slaughter many of the Filipino faithful. At the height of the crisis, Jaime Cardinal Sin asked all religious orders to pray, and mandated perpetual Eucharistic adoration by all contemplative communities throughout the islands until the end of the conflict. Many have testified to the miraculous Eucharistic and Marian nature of the peaceful resolution in the Philippines. The Filipino people knew that all struggle against evil must be waged primarily with prayer. Their hearts were open. They heard the call of their Shepherd and responded.

When we come to adore our Eucharistic Lord, we too must prepare to receive the graces He longs to give us by our openness and our emptying. The more we empty ourselves, the more God is able to fill us.

When we come to adore the Heart of Jesus exposed in the Eucharist, we should also expose our hearts, the innermost heart of our souls, and let the sanctifying power of the Sacred Heart heal, strengthen, and fill our hearts anew.

We should begin adoration by stripping ourselves of our own desires and concerns, and let the Sacred Heart fill our hearts with His desires, priorities, petitions.

The more emptied we are of our desires before the exposed Heart of Jesus, the more He truly fills us with His graces, His intentions, His work for the Kingdom of God and for the Triumph.

As a mode of meditation, we can begin our own adoration with words similar to these:

> "O my precious Lord Jesus, as I sit before You now, my heart is very still. I feel Your peace flow through my heart, my soul, my veins, my capillaries, my entire self. I am Your happy and willing captive, dear Jesus. Every one of my breaths long for You. I feel the bonds of Your love and

mercy wrapped around my soul. My body may still be here on this earth, dear Lord, but my soul is bound to You."

Can we not hear our Eucharistic Jesus respond to such a humble and a childlike invitation with these words:

"My child, listen to Me now as I call to you. Come into the shelter of My Heart and rest. You are beginning to understand what it is to be stripped of this world in which you live. For these moments, you are with me entirely. Your body, your mind, your soul are here before Me, with Me, in Me. Linger here, My child. Let My Love and Mercy flood the chambers of your heart as you rest in Me and I in you. Understand that this is why I stay here, I stay here in My Eucharistic presence, so that you and all My children can come to Me, can rest in Me, can find shelter and refreshment, strength and courage to go on and continue to do My work in this world.

"Your heart feels comfort in Me and I in you. We are joined, Heart to heart. My blood flows in you, My body feeds and nourishes you. Your cells carry My Mark, as I touch every cell in your body.

"See the changes I have made in you. As you relinquish more of yourself to Me, I mold you and unite you closer to My Heart's desire for you.

"Do not grow impatient. See how much I have changed you over the recent past. See how much you have had to relinquish. Now you are coming to know true freedom. Freedom from this world and union of your will to Mine.

"You will understand a small portion of this union in your life here on earth; you will understand much more in the world to come.

"For now, rest with Me. Bask in My Love and Mercy. Wait for Me, watch for Me. Be still and silent so that you may continue to hear My voice. Trust in Me."

And our response, in the words of a child:

"O my Jesus, I am nothing on my own and can do nothing without You. Please continue to show me those areas of myself that I need to relinquish. Thank You, precious Lord, for all Your mercy, graces, and blessings You have given me since I began my journey with You. I pray to be continually filled with Your strength, courage, and peace so that I may continue

on the path You wish me to walk. Please
keep me in the light of Your love."

In responding to Our Lord's great outpouring of
His love for us, what are we to do in practical terms?
What are we called to accomplish as Marian apostles?

First of all, it is clear that the world is in great
need of Eucharistic adoration. Let us consider the
following possibility. In honor of, and in reparation
for, the seven sorrows of the Immaculate Heart of
Mary, bishops could choose the seven most vibrant
parishes of their dioceses, the parishes that would
be most quick to accept this call, and establish Eucharistic perpetual adoration there. Remember
Abraham pleading with the Lord in the Old Testament, asking him to save Sodom if there be but "ten
just men" in that city. Tragically, ten righteous souls
could not be found, and thus Sodom was destroyed.
But here is an invitation to seven parishes to grow in
sanctity and to intercede for the city, for the diocese,
for the Church, and for the world. "Lord, for seven
good parishes," we pray, "will you spare us?" Surely
we can find seven places in each diocese where the
Eucharistic Lord is welcomed wholeheartedly. And
if a diocese is larger, if it is an archdiocese with very
large numbers of faithful, are we not called to be more
generous? Could we find twelve parishes to crown
our Mother with twelve stars of adoration for her
Son? And if we are shepherds of archdioceses of great
dimension, could we strive to offer fifteen parishes,

one in honor of each decade of the Rosary? Mother Teresa of Calcutta once said that when communism was just beginning to fall in Russia she prayed to the Blessed Mother, "Mother, if you let me into Russia, I will give you fifteen houses of the Missionaries of Charity, one for each decade of the Rosary." Within a year and a half of making that prayer, she had already established thirteen houses in the former Soviet Union. Can we do less in our own lands for the sublime fruit of Eucharistic adoration?

Bishops and priests may ask, "Is it not better for this desire for Perpetual Adoration to come from the people?" Yes, in many places throughout the world this initiative has come from the people, responding to Heaven's grace. Yet there is a special grace when a father, when a shepherd, says, "I would like you, my children, to adore Jesus in the Eucharist." Often the lay faithful hesitate to ask for adoration because they are unsure if the shepherds want it, wondering if it will add to their pastors' already full responsibilities. How often have they battled amongst themselves, saying, "You ask Father." "No, you ask Father." "No, you ask Father if we can have adoration." But what joy and happiness comes when the father himself asks his children to respond to this great gift, for then all doubts evaporate and the floodgates of grace are opened. Then the people respond: "My bishop has asked me, my priest has asked me, my shepherd has asked me, to adore Jesus. Happily, I will."

Therefore, let us take risks, let us be daring, let us be bold for the Eucharist, and we shall see the immeasurable fruits. Remember what the Lord said and did during the discourses on the Bread of Life in the sixth chapter of John's Gospel. Jesus taught the people about the new "manna" come down from Heaven, which is Himself. This occurred immediately after Jesus fed the 5000 with the miraculous multiplication of loaves and fishes. The crowds loved the miracles, but when Jesus told them that they must eat his flesh and drink his blood if they wished to have life within them, many of the disciples murmured, "This is a hard saying! How can anyone endure it?" Many of His followers left Him at that moment. Jesus then turned to the Twelve and asked them, "Do you also want to leave me?" Simon Peter answered Him, "Lord, to whom shall we go? You have the words of eternal life."

Jesus was always willing to be a sign of contradiction, and we too must be willing to be a sign of contradiction for Him and for the adoration of his Eucharistic Heart —to serve as He served, to teach as He taught, to call the faithful to feed upon this Bread which is the source of eternal life (Jn 6:58). Like St. Peter, the Catholic faithful will respond with enthusiasm, as evidenced by the numerous parishes throughout the world where the Blessed Sacrament is exposed for Eucharistic adoration, a practice which is bearing an abundant harvest in conversions, renewal of parish life, and increased vocations to the priesthood and consecrated religious life.

Admittedly, there are certain cultures where Eucharistic Adoration is new. People will sometimes say, "We do not feel worthy to have Jesus exposed through the day." The answer to this objection is, "You are right, we are not worthy, but all the more reason why we need our Eucharistic Jesus and His graces showered upon our people through adoration." We are unworthy to receive Him internally in Holy Communion—*Dominum non sum dignus*—yet this is not an impediment but rather a call to reception of the Sacrament. None of us is worthy to receive Jesus in this sacrament, which is all the more reason why we *must* receive Him. Similarly, regarding adoration, our very unworthiness is the very reason why we need to adore Him.

Because adoration of Jesus is at the heart of the *missio* of the universal Church, it must become a universal practice. If for cultural or other reasons there is an initial hesitancy on the part of the faithful, we should listen to these words of Jesus: "Be not afraid." Perfect love casts out fear (cf. 1 Jn 4:18). With gentle firmness we must call the flock to "aim higher" as St. Maximilian Kolbe tells us. If we were to allow ourselves to be restricted by the voices of fear or misunderstanding or lukewarmness, we would reduce the evangelical work of the Church to only those things which are commonly acceptable, to those things which disturb no one, to those things which are not "a hard saying." Instead, we must have confidence that the faithful will rise to the challenge and come to understand the celestial power of Eucharistic adoration.

Thus, the Eucharistic Adoration of Jesus must become transcultural. Have confidence in the faithful to see the inestimable power and grace of our Eucharistic Jesus. In this mode of universality, I would like to end with a prayer, a prayer that perhaps could be used before our Eucharistic Jesus in commencing Adoration. This prayer in many ways resembles more of an Eastern prayer known such as the 'Jesus prayer.' It could be used throughout different cultures in preparing the heart to be open to our Eucharistic Lord:

"My child, breathe in My Spirit and breathe out your will; breathe in My Spirit and breathe out your will. This is when I come to dwell within your heart, soul, mind, and body. Release all that keeps you apart from Me, and breathe in My Spirit to fill those places that were once filled with your will and which kept you away from Me. I wish to fill you with My Breath of Life. I wish to dwell in every part of your heart and soul. I wish to give you thoughts of Me that will help you grow, to understand, to know what you are meant to know.

"Breathe in My Spirit, breathe out your will. I am in you and you are in Me. I am in My Father and My Father is in Me.

Therefore My child, My Father and I are with you as you breathe in My Spirit. Be one with your Triune God. Breathe in My Spirit, breathe out your will. This is union. I am with you always."

May our Lady Coredemptrix, the Woman of Cana, who forever directs us to "do whatever he tells you" (Jn 2:5), keep our hearts fixed always on her Eucharistic Son, and keep us company in the adoration of the Most Blessed Sacrament, where the Heart of Christ fills our hearts with his own divine life and divine love. Amen.

Chapter 3

A Spiritual Call to Action for All Hearts Consecrated to the Immaculate Heart

"A Marian Remnant"

We who are consecrated as "Totus Tuus" servants and slaves of our Mother Coredemptrix must now begin anew our prayer and labor for the Triumph of the Immaculate Heart of Mary! Even with the eventual definition of the last Marian Dogma, members of *Vox Populi* and all hearts consecrated to the Immaculate Heart of Mary must continue to participate as a Marian family, a Marian remnant, in bringing forth all components of the great Triumph of our Mother, which leads to the Eucharistic Reign of the Most Sacred Heart of Jesus.

We have a great responsibility, one which will not be easy to fulfill, considering the state of the world and the many storms which rock the Church. We would do well to keep in mind the courage of Peter when he was commanded by Our Lord Jesus to step out onto the water. Peter obeyed and at first he remained afloat, because he kept his eyes fixed on Christ. The moment Peter began to focus on the startling fact that he, himself, was walking on water, he took his eyes from Jesus and put them onto himself, and began to sink.

My brothers and sisters, we have the same invitation. Our Immaculate Mother is asking us, in a certain sense, to "walk on water." Our call is simply obedience. If we keep our eyes fixed on Jesus Christ, we can walk on water. If we keep our eyes focused on ourselves, we will very quickly sink. Perhaps our minds will at times argue that to walk on water is irrational. We must remember that the head can distract the heart, and therefore in order to do its proper function in the body, the mind must be in right relationship with the other faculties of our human nature. The call of the Triumph of the Immaculate Heart is not anti-intellectual. Our consecration is not just a consecration of heart, or a consecration of the mind; it is a consecration of *both* head and heart. The intellect is a tremendous gift from God, but it must always be on guard against an intellectual pride that leads the soul away from obedience and charity of the heart: to God, to our Mother, to our Holy Father. Full participation for the Triumph is a call of truth which leads to a call of charity in action, for truth is inseparable from love.

We are charged with the responsibility of being bearers of the truth about the Dogma, and about other components complementary to the Triumph. What are some of the conditions for praying and working for the Triumph of the Immaculate Heart leading to the Reign of the Sacred and Eucharistic Heart of Jesus? Perseverance, loyalty, and obedience to the Immaculate Heart of Mary and to Pope John Paul II. We are all aware of the reality of division which is growing within the Church today. To remain loyal to Pope John Paul II will become increasingly difficult in many parts of the world, and thus we are faced with the need for increasing self sacrifice, particularly a willingness for a sacrifice of reputation. In order to meet this challenge, we must daily make proper spiritual preparation for the battle that lies ahead, because the struggle for souls and for the life of the Church necessarily involves suffering.

We must put on our spiritual armor, "the armor of God" described in Ephesians 6: "Stand therefore, having girded your loins with truth, and having put on the breastplate of righteousness, and having shod your feet with the equipment of the gospel of peace; above all taking the shield of faith, with which you can quench the flaming darts of the evil one. And take the helmet of salvation, and the sword of the Spirit, which is the word of God"(Eph 6:14-17).

Our ultimate protection and source of strength is the Eucharist, not only the reception of the Eucharist at Holy Mass, but also Eucharistic Adoration. Regarding the latter we should develop a spirituality of "keeping watch" with the Lord. Scripture cautions us that during Our Lord's agony in the garden, the apostles were sorely tested. Because they were frightened and weary, because they had not fully prepared their hearts, the Apostles were not able to stay awake with Jesus, supporting him in prayer (Lk 22:45-46). The Apostles themselves needed the spiritual preparation of prayer to be able to follow Jesus into the midst of persecution and threats, and even unto death. Yet they slept.

My brothers and sisters in the Immaculate Heart, we must not sleep. During these times when the Church is approaching a period of purification (and as the late Fulton Sheen foresaw, even an "ecclesial crucifixion"), we must not allow our hearts to be distracted by anything other than this aim—to be spiritually prepared to follow Pope John Paul II under all conditions, for the Triumph of the Immaculate Heart. If we try to stay awake by our own strength we will certainly drift into sleep. If we keep spiritual vigilance by the power of grace flowing from adoring the living presence of Jesus in the Eucharist, and by the love of his Sacred Heart, then we will be awake. Our hearts are like a garden into which the Lord has come seeking the comfort of His friends. We must cultivate, water and weed this garden. Our humanity is a reality that God has sanctified by the Incarnation and Redemption, and therefore, when we hear a call from Our Lord Jesus, it is not a call in opposition to our humanity, but rather a call to sanctify our humanity to the fullest by submitting every aspect of our being to the Divine.

Let us place ourselves for a moment in the Garden of Gethsemane.

> "The air is fragrant with the perfume of flowers, and the night is still, and we feel a great sadness and loneliness building in our hearts. We see You now, Lord, entering the garden. You kneel before a rock and lean Your weight upon the cold stone. Your face is so sad, and drops of sweat and blood fall from Your brow. You say to us: 'Child, My friends have abandoned Me, they do not know what the next few hours will bring. I have asked them to wait and pray with Me, but they sleep instead. They do not know that My hour has come. They are not prepared. Prepare your hearts, dear children. Many will abandon you, but Your Jesus will not. Watch with Me, My little ones, stay with Me in the garden of your hearts. Do not fear, I am with you always. Keep your hearts awake to the sound of My voice calling to you. Come to Me, My heart waits for you.'"

Jesus experienced the abandonment of many of those closest to Him—apostles, disciples, those He considered "family" (except, of course, His own co-redeeming mother). We too must be ready to have those closest to us threaten abandonment because of our choice to follow the Vicar of Christ today. Jesus says to each one of us: "He who loves father or mother more than me is not worthy of me; and he who loves son or daughter more than me is not worthy of me; and he who does not take his cross and follow me is not worthy of me. He who loses his life for my sake will find it" (Mt 10:37-39).

But where will we find the strength for trials such as these? We must prepare the most innermost tabernacles of our heart so that if we some day find ourselves in a situation where we cannot be before Our Lord in the Most Blessed Sacrament, we can still go to Him in the innermost tabernacles of our heart. In similar fashion, Saint Teresa of Avila writes about the "interior castle," and Saint Catherine of Siena speaks about her "interior cell." The classic teaching of authentic Catholic spirituality, so beautifully articulated by Blessed Elizabeth of the Trinity and many other spiritual giants, tells us that the life of the Trinity dwells in the hearts of the just. All of these remind us that there is a small chapel within each of our hearts in grace, and an altar where the most beautiful monstrance that we have ever seen contains within it Our Eucharistic Jesus. There is never a time, there is no situation and no place on earth where we cannot come to Him in the tabernacle of our hearts. If the availability of Eucharistic Adoration, or if the reception of Jesus in the Eucharist becomes increasingly scarce, we must not fear, for Jesus will always remain in the tabernacle of our hearts, strengthening and sustaining us for every sacrifice that He personally and individually calls us to.

Saint Paul tells us: "But you are not in the flesh, you are in the Spirit, if the Spirit of God really dwells in you. Any one who does not have the Spirit of Christ does not belong to Him. But if Christ is in you, although your bodies are dead because of sin, your spirits are alive because of righteousness. If the Spirit of him who raised Jesus from the dead dwells in you, he who raised Christ Jesus from the dead will give life to your mortal bodies also through his Spirit who dwells in you" (Rom 8:9-11). And again from St. Paul, "Do you not know that your body is a temple of the Holy Spirit within you, which you have from God? You are not your own; you were bought with a price. So glorify God in your body" (1 Cor 6:19-20).

Our Lord tells us: "I am the good shepherd; I know my own and my own know me" (Jn 10:14). Thus, we must prepare our hearts to recognize the voice of the Good Shepherd speaking through His Vicar Pope John Paul II, for there may come a time when it will be difficult to distinguish this voice of truth from false and illusory voices. Our Eternal Father in Heaven has created a hierarchical Church, and thus our fidelity to the Vicar of Christ is fidelity to Christ Himself, who renders all glory and honor to the Father.

Carriers of the Love
and Mercy of the Sacred Heart

Continuing our meditation, let us hear the voice of Jesus speaking to our hearts, inviting us to open our hearts entirely, without limit, without any fear, to His Most Sacred Heart:

"I am the Resurrection and the Life. Come to Me and I shall give you new life. Come, rest in My Sacred Heart. Shed all your troubles and allow Me to rejuvenate you with My love and mercy. Allow Me to lift the burdens from your hearts and fill you with My peace that surpasses anything you know here on Earth. Never be afraid to come to Me and open your hearts. I know the burdens of your hearts and minds intimately. Share them with Me. Trust in Me. I will not forsake you or abandon you. You are My beloved children, the joy of My Heart. Trust in Me; come let Me give you new life in My Heart, your refuge from the pains and troubles of this world. Here you shall find strength and hope, joy and peace, love and mercy. With these gifts I wish to give you, you will be my carriers, my instruments of love and mercy to share with your brothers and sisters who have lost their

way in the darkness of despair. Lead them
back to Me, My children. Let My love in
you be a light for all to see. You are light
for all to see."

Our Lord knows our minds and hearts intimately,
better than we know them ourselves. We might then
ask the question of why the omniscient Jesus, who
knows all of our concerns, desires us to specifically
and intimately share our greatest concerns and desires with Him? He does so because our sharing of
our greatest burdens manifests our trust in Him,
deepens our relationship with Him as a child opening its heart to its father. And as our trust in Him
grows, we are more able to receive the graces He longs
to give us.

Often in family life, a father will realize that one
of his elder children is carrying some private burden.
But because of the maturity of the child, the father
also knows he has to wait until the child comes to
him. The father may try to probe gently, or find op-
portunities to bring it up in conversation, but if the
child is not ready to reveal his problem, repeated efforts to investigate will just harden the child's heart.
And so the father, in a patient wait that is truly pain-
ful, waits for the child to come to him. What joy he
feels when at last the child comes and says, "Father, I
wish to speak of a great burden in my heart." Then
you have the joyous combination of release of the
burden by the child, coupled with the grace and the

wisdom of the father. The father's love is freed to flow to the child, and the child grows in trust of his father. Our Abba Father in heaven calls us to do the same with Jesus. The Father wants us to tell Him, through His Divine Son, what is *truly burdening our hearts,* not simply to say what we think He would like to hear.

The Sacred Heart of Jesus tells us that He is our ultimate refuge: "Come to me, all who labor and are heavy laden, and I will give you rest. Take my yoke upon you, and learn from me; for I am gentle and lowly in heart, and you will find rest for your souls. For my yoke is easy, and my burden is light" (Mt 11:28-30).

Do we take the words of the Sacred Heart of Jesus seriously, or do we dismiss the words of Jesus as a well intentioned, pious statement? When things go wrong in our efforts for the Church or our families, do we fly first to the refuge of Jesus in the Blessed Sacrament, or do we attempt to solve our problems and carry our burdens on our own? Perhaps a certain pride prevents us from going immediately to our Father, or perhaps a kind of immaturity, like the child who wants to do it by himself in order to feel "grown-up." Or perhaps we are fearful and ashamed. Perhaps we are afraid that the Abba isn't really the loving father He says He is. Some of us have not been gifted with a loving earthly father and find it difficult to conceive of the loving and intimate Fatherhood of God. Yet all of us have met examples of outstanding human fathers, and we should see them as reflections of the infinite love of our Abba, Father. We should look especially to the extraordinary and efficacious example of St. Joseph, who in so many ways is a human icon of the Heavenly Abba.

Mercy and Justice

God is Love. But He is Justice as well as Love. Archbishop Fulton Sheen once wrote that God's justice must intervene in history at some point, because He will not permit evil to go on devouring souls forever. Thus, we must understand that the justice of God is ultimately *mercy*. Our Blessed Mother has told us at the Church-approved Marian Apparitions at Fatima and Akita and so many others, that unless the world converts, a time of great trial, a tragic climax of darkness and destruction, is approaching for mankind. Unless we run home to our Abba, the Father of All Mankind we will have to live with the consequences of our sins. The choice is ours.

Each of us is called to be a carrier of the light of Jesus to those who have turned from the light to darkness. At times of darkness, one candle alone suffices to light an entire room. We are called to be such candles, witnessing to the mercy that all human beings can find in the Eucharistic Jesus, if they would only come to Him. We need not be afraid of this task. We need not think that we are called to convert the whole world by our own little efforts. It is always wondrous to see how God can use "nothings" and make something pleasing to God from them! Let us all see ourselves as a *"Nihil Mariae,"* a "nothing of Mary," who in our nothingness and weakness can be used as strong instruments of God. Is this not the spirit of the Magnificat (cf. Lk 1:42ff)?

It is Jesus who lights the wicks of our souls and sustains the flame. And even if the number of repentant souls is not enough to prevent the chastisement and purification of the world, we must understand with a certain maturity that we live in a blessed, decisive moment in the history of the Church. Our Lady, as a good mother, has communicated the urgency of our need for special protection, special graces, special solicitude for the state of our souls in these times. How well has she been heeded? What has been the response of our people? Modern man is strongly influenced by the climate of materialism, and by the pride which says "I can solve any problem if I just have enough knowledge and power." It is difficult for modern man to admit that there are no purely human solutions to the present, dangerous state of the world, and especially difficult for people of the affluent West to arrive at this point of humility.

We should ask ourselves if the conditional warnings given through the approved Marian apparitions of the 19th and 20th centuries are as unrealistic as some would like to think. Is chastisement something new in salvation history? Do we not have the precedent in the Old Testament of the great plagues, exiles, and destruction which fell upon the people of

God when they persisted in sin and refused to listen to the prophets? Is it also not true that the places where the Church is undergoing its greatest opposition from its own members, where faith is becoming very weak and apostasy is spreading, are precisely the places where there has not yet been a great trial for the Church? God knows that in the end suffering calls us back to a sense of reality, to truth, to Him. Persecutions always bear a great harvest of conversions for the Mystical Body.

A person from the West once asked a Bishop from Eastern Europe, "Why hasn't the Church in the West gone through direct persecution in a very explicit way, for example, losing jobs for the faith, being imprisoned for the faith, losing property and possessions and even our lives for the faith?" The Eastern Bishop replied, "Because the Church in the West has not been so blessed. But your time is coming."

We know that, historically, the Church is purified and strengthened by trials. If difficult times are ahead, let us remember that in conforming ourselves to Christ we are called to live out in some way His Passion and Death. But remember always that if we are conformed to the sufferings of Christ, then we will also take part in the Resurrection of Christ. At the Ascension, Jesus promises us, "Behold I am with you always, until the end of time" (Mt 28:20).

Let us ponder, in the form of a meditation, what Our Lord might say to us as He longs for our hearts to be completely and intimately united to His Own

Resurrected and Eucharistic Heart, that through our intimate, heart-to-Heart union with Him, we may ascend and soar to heaven with Him.

The Jesus of the Ascension says to each one of us:

> "Surrender yourselves to Me, let Me hold your hearts next to Mine. I desire that there be no separation between your hearts and Mine. Ask with your heart that anything that separates you from Me be removed. Let the desire of your heart be for Me and I shall fill you with every grace and blessing. Pray with love in your hearts, dear children, and these prayers shall ascend like lights of life to My Father's throne in Heaven. When you pray with love in your heart, and your soul abandoned to My care, your prayers ring throughout Heaven and are joined by those who have gone before you.
>
> "Remember, I am with you always."

During the great battles of the Church Militant, we must never forget both the great intercessory power of the Church Triumphant, and the mighty intercessory power of the glorious choirs of angels. How sad it is that so many have lost daily devotion to the saints, whose living human examples remind us that heroic sanctity, even unto death and martyrdom, is truly possible for us. We should therefore fly with great confidence to the saints in times of difficulty, pray with renewed vigor to our patron saints, and have special devotion and recourse to the saint of the day, as found in the liturgical calendar of the Church.

Think of just a few examples from the countless witnesses who have gone before us: St. Ignatius of Antioch, who longed to become "the wheat of God crushed in the lion's mouth," to be united with the Eucharistic Jesus; St. Polycarp, who said to those igniting the fire which consumed his body, "You are starting a temporal fire for me, but beware, because you are starting an eternal fire for yourselves." Think also of Saints Felix and Adauctus. Felix was a priest in the early Church who was horribly tortured by the worst possible methods, and yet he went to his martyrdom like a lamb, in the midst of a great crowd. The humble gentleness with which Felix accepted his sufferings moved and inspired the heart of a member of the crowd who was not Christian. The man cried out, "I am ready to accept Jesus, the Christ, the God of this man, because of the peace of this man as he goes to his death." And with that, this unknown man was taken out of the crowd and killed alongside of Felix. Because we do not know his name, the martyrology simply refers to him as "Adauctus," the additional one. Remember also Saint Lawrence the Deacon, who told his torturers as they slowly burned him alive, "This side is done. You can turn me over now." And the young Saint Tarcissius, the Eucharistic martyr, who gave up his life in defense of the Eucharist rather than permit desecration of the Blessed Sacrament.

These people are not legends, my brothers and sisters; they are *living human testimonies* to the truth that *we* can offer all things, even our very lives if so called, in defense of the Eucharist. It has been done before by those who cooperate with God's perfect and all sustaining grace, and, if need be, it can be done again by us, with the help of God's grace.

We must also renew our devotion to our patron saints. Those saints after whom we are named have been given a special power of intercession for us in our vocations and states in life. I also want to remind you of the two great patron saints of *Vox Populi Mariae Mediatrici*. Firstly, there is Saint Joseph, the spouse of Mary and Patron of the Universal Church. Think of his awesome responsibility. St. Joseph, a fallen though redeemed man, was charged with the task of caring as Foster-Father for Jesus, God-made-man, and for his wife, Mary, God's greatest masterpiece. We might underestimate this by saying, "Oh yes, but he knew God would take care of him. He knew God would give him the grace to fulfill his duty as head of the Holy Family, even when threatened with death by Herod." He obeyed. He made each step of the journey in *faith*.

What keeps you and me, then, from having the same trust? We, too, are given the necessary grace by God to fulfill every aspect of our providential duties in life. And yet, we oftentimes fall short of the faith, trust and obedience that Joseph exemplified. We must see Saint Joseph as "our common foster-father," who exemplifies sanctity in humility and hidden holiness, second only to his Immaculate Spouse. All efforts of *Vox Populi* and all efforts of a Marian Remnant of hearts consecrated to the Immaculate Heart must be submitted to the powerful intercession of the "Guardian of the Redeemer." Saint Teresa of Avila and Saint Francis de Sales both testify that they never asked anything of St. Joseph, "the just man," without receiving it. We must invoke his aid especially in times of temptation and opposition to our apostolate for the Triumph. It was not by accident that he appeared during the sixth apparition at Fatima, blessing the world with the Child Jesus, thus underlining his crucial intercessory role for the Immaculate Heart and for her Triumph.

The second great patron of *Vox Populi Mariae Mediatrici* is Saint Catherine of Siena. This third order lay woman had an unquestioning loyalty to the Holy Father, and was willing to follow him regardless of geography. We recall especially her persistence in bringing the Holy Father back to Rome from what was called the "Avignon exile." St. Catherine personifies lay support for the Vicar of Christ under any and all conditions. We must capture St. Catherine's love and respect for the Holy Father and exercise it for our own beloved Totus Tuus Pope.

And in general, we must also increase our devotion to the Holy Angels. The angels are God's messengers who bring understanding, strength, and perseverance to the human conscience in leading us to our heavenly home. We must return to prayer and devotion to our guardian angels. We must invoke Our Mother, the sovereign Mistress of the angels, to send her holy legions and in a special way, the Archangel St. Michael, Prince of the Angels, that under his command they may defend us from the evil spirits, encounter them on every side, resist their bold attacks, and drive them hence into the abyss of everlasting woe.

The holy angels do battle on levels that we as simply humans cannot see. Because the angelic intellect is so far beyond ours, because it does not depend on materiality, it is immediate, infused intellect, and it serves the holy angels in their providential role as an indispensable force for the Church.

Let us properly venerate and invoke the first three choirs of holy angels, who contemplate God in His divine essence and goodness:

> 1. the Seraphim, who "excel in what is the supreme excellence of all in being united to God Himself;"
>
> 2. the Cherubim, who "know the Divine secrets supereminently;"
>
> 3. the Thrones, who "are raised up so as to be the familiar recipients of God in themselves."

Let us properly venerate and invoke the next three choirs of holy angels, who govern the universe in conformity with the Divine will:

> 4. the Dominations, who "appoint those things which are to be done;"
> 5. the Powers, who "order how what has been commanded or decided to be done can be carried out by others;"
> 6. the Virtues, who "give the power of carrying out what is to be done."

Let us properly venerate and invoke the last three choirs of holy angels, who execute divine orders for the good of the Church and the world:

> 7. the Principalities, who are the "generals and officers... in the execution of any action;"
> 8. the Archangels, who "announce the highest things... For this reason the Archangel Gabriel was sent to the Virgin Mary;"
> 9. the Angels, who "simply execute what is to be done." (St. Thomas Aquinas, *Summa Theologica*, Q 108,112)

We must become more and more attentive to the promptings of our guardian angels as they protect, warn, and guide us through the spiritual battlefield of today. Imagine the waste of celestial providence and power when we do not invite our guardian angel, a being more highly created than we are, a being more intelligent than we are, to help us each day. Once again, we must remember that Heaven will force nothing upon us. It respects our freedom; therefore we must ask for these graces and heavenly assistance.

Let us also look to the three great archangels: St. Michael, the angel of the Father; St. Gabriel, the angel of the Son; and St. Raphael, the angel of the Holy Spirit, who lead us in this great work of the Triumph and help us to be willing, fighting members for Our Lady's spiritual army. Let us never underestimate the grave significance of this battle, the historic battle between the Woman and the serpent (cf. Gen 3:15) which climactically rages in our own historical moment, nor be naive about its seriousness and possibility of danger and fatalities. Our call is not to take on the forces of the adversary and his unholy legions on our own. In this great battle, every level of the Kingdom of God is engaged: Jesus and His Mother; the Church Triumphant - the holy angels and the saints; the Church Suffering - the souls in Purgatory; and the Church Militant - the pilgrim Church on earth. This is a definitive battle against the forces of Satan and against all those who join him in his efforts against Jesus and Jesus' Vicar on earth, Pope John Paul II. The Church's ultimate victory is assured. Yet we must always keep in mind and heart that count-less individual souls hang in the balance.

Let us consider the Church-approved message of Our Lady of Akita, Japan which has revealed to us the challenges that lie ahead. In the final public message of the Blessed Virgin to the visionary Sister Agnes Sasagawa, Our Lady said on October 13, 1973, the anniversary of the great Fatima apparition and solar miracle:

> "Pray very much the prayers of the Rosary. I alone am able to save you from the calamities that approach. Those who place their confidence in me will be saved.
>
> "My dear daughter, listen well to what I have to say to you. You will inform your superior. As I told you, if men do not repent and better themselves, the Father will inflict a terrible punishment on all humanity. It will be a punishment greater than the deluge, such as one will never have seen before. Fire will fall from the sky and will wipe out a great part of humanity, the good as well as the bad, sparing neither priests nor faithful. The survivors will find themselves so desolate that they will envy the dead. The only arms that will remain for you will be the Rosary and Sign left by My Son. Each day recite the prayers of

the Rosary. With the Rosary, pray for the Pope, the bishops, and the priests.

"The work of the devil will infiltrate the Church in such a way that one will see cardinals opposing cardinals, bishops against other bishops. The priests who venerate Me will be scorned and opposed by their confreres... churches and altars sacked, the Church will be full of those who accept compromises, and the demon will press many priests and consecrated souls to leave the service of the Lord. The demon will be especially implacable against souls consecrated to God. The thought of the loss of so many souls is the cause of my sadness. If sins increase in number and gravity, there will be no longer pardon for them.

"With courage, speak to your superior. He will know how to encourage each one of you to pray and to accomplish works of reparation."

Obviously, there should be an appropriate respect for all messages approved by the Church, and thus I would encourage you to read our Holy Father's encyclical, *Dives in Misericordia*, On Divine Mercy. In the last section of that encyclical, the Holy Father likewise alludes to the possibility of a great purification of the earth. The threat of an "immense danger which threatens humanity" is real enough, and for this reason the Pope exhorts us to pray, so that our realistic recognition about the difficulties and darkness of the times be "continually transformed into an ardent prayer" invoking the Mercy of God upon all mankind:

> "However, at no time and in no historical period — *especially at a moment as critical as our own* — can the Church forget the prayer that is a cry for the mercy of God amid the many forms of evil which weigh upon humanity and threaten it... And, like the prophets, let us appeal to that love which has maternal characteristics and which, like a mother, follows each of her children, each lost sheep, even if they should number millions, even if in the world evil should prevail over goodness, even if contemporary humanity should deserve a new 'flood' on account of its sins, as once the generation of Noah did... and if any of our contemporaries does not share the faith and hope which lead me, as a servant of Christ and steward of the mysteries of God, to implore God's mercy for humanity in this hour of history, let him at least try to understand the reason for my concern. It is dictated by love for man, for all that is human and

which, according to the intuitions of many of our contemporaries, is threatened by an immense danger... The mystery of Christ... also obliges me to proclaim mercy as God's merciful love... it likewise obliges me to have recourse to that mercy and to beg for it in this difficult, critical phase of the history of the Church and of the world, as we approach the end of the second millennium... Let us have recourse to God through Christ, mindful of the words of Mary's *Magnificat*, which proclaim mercy 'from generation to generation.' Let us implore mercy for the present generation" (*Dives in Misericordia*, n.15).

The Holy Father is calling us to run to the merciful Heart of Jesus. In another place in the encyclical he writes:

"The Church lives an authentic life when she professes and proclaims mercy—the most stupendous attribute of the Creator and of the Redeemer—and when she brings people close to the sources of the Savior's mercy, of which she is the trustee and dispenser. Of great significance in this area is constant meditation on the Word of God, and above all conscious and mature participation *in the*

Eucharist and *in the sacrament of Penance or Reconciliation.* The Eucharist brings us ever nearer to that *love* which is more powerful than death. 'For as we eat this bread and drink this cup,' we proclaim not only the death of the Redeemer but also His resurrection, 'until He comes' in glory" (*Dives in Misericordia*, n.13).

Our victorious Saviour reminds us: "In the world you will have tribulation; but be of good cheer, I have overcome the world, " (Jn 16:33).

Let us listen to the words that our merciful Jesus could speak to us, *"cor ad cor"*:

"In the time of what seems like hopeless and helpless despair, My remnant, those who stay close to Me, who know that I am the Source of their strength, these devoted ones will be brilliant lights in the greatest darkness the world has ever known. Those who come to Me in their greatest pain and sorrow and offer to Me all that burdens them, trusting in My Love and Mercy, I will hold in My Heart. Much is to come, much is to be endured, stay close My sweet ones, I am with you in your greatest trials. Trust in Me. I am your strength and the light to lead you through the darkness. I, your Jesus, am the Source of All Love and Mercy."

Marching Orders For Our Lady's Army

What is the call to order for our Mother's co-hearts? It is nothing less than that which issues from the great prophesy of Genesis 3:15, where again we are told that from the beginning there would be a great historic battle between the Woman and the serpent. "I will put enmity between you and the woman, between your seed and her seed." The battle has been going on in various stages throughout human history. We must expect that as the role of this Woman reaches a dramatic climax, the adversary's malice will also be manifested with unprecedented force. During the decisive moments of this battle we are to obey the words of Scripture to "Be not afraid" (Jn 6:20). This is the time for courage, and for increased efforts for the salvation of souls.

Listen to the piercing prophesy at Fatima of "Our Lady of the Rosary." During the crucial apparition of July 13, 1917, our Blessed Mother said to the world through the children of Fatima:

> "I want you to come here on the 13th of next month, to continue to pray the Rosary every day in honor of Our Lady of the Rosary, in order to obtain peace in the world and the end of the war, because only she can help you...

"Sacrifice yourselves for sinners, and say many times, especially whenever you make some sacrifice: O Jesus, it is for love of You, for the conversion of sinners, and in reparation for the sins committed against the Immaculate Heart of Mary."

When Our Lady spoke these concluding words she opened her hands, as she had done during the two previous months. The rays of light which came from her hands seemed to penetrate the earth, and, in the words of Lucia:

"We saw, as it were, a sea of fire. Plunged in this fire were demons and souls in human form, like transparent burning embers, all blackened or burnished bronze, floating about in the conflagration, now raised into the air by the flames that issued within themselves together with great clouds of smoke, now falling back on every side like sparks in huge fires, without weight or equilibrium, amid shrieks and groans of pain and despair, which horrified us and made us tremble with fear (It must have been this sight which caused me to cry out, as people say they heard me). The demons could be distinguished by their terrifying and repellent likeness to frightful and unknown animals, black and transparent like burning coals. Terrified and as if to plead for succor, we looked up at Our Lady, who said to us, so kindly and sadly:

'You have seen hell where the souls of poor sinners go. To save them, God wishes to establish in the world devotion to my Immaculate Heart. If what I say to you is done, many souls will be saved and there will be peace. The war is going to end; but if people do not cease offending God, a worse one will break out during the pontificate of Pius XI. When you see a night illuminated by an unknown light, know that this is a great sign given you by God that He is about to punish the world for its crimes, by means of war, famine, and persecutions of the Church and the Holy Father.

'To prevent this, I shall come to ask for the consecration of Russia to my Immaculate Heart, and the Communion of Reparation on the First Saturdays. If my requests are heeded, Russia will be converted, and there will be peace; if not, she will spread her errors throughout the world, causing wars and persecutions of the Church. The good will be martyred, the Holy Father will have much to suffer, various nations will be annihilated. In the

end, my Immaculate Heart will Triumph.
The Holy Father will consecrate Russia to
me, and she will be converted, and a period of peace will be granted to the whole
world'" (*Sr. Lucia's Memoirs*).

How should we respond to this great Marian
warning for our twentieth century? First of all, it is
conditional, just as the plagues of the Old Testament
were conditional. If humanity responds, the purification is mitigated or even avoided altogether. Sadly,
at the time of 1917, the response of the world was not
significant enough to prevent a second world war.
Secondly, our Mother promises victory, and she
makes this promise at the end of her description of
the difficulties that will come. Clearly, we cannot take
the last line of the message—the Triumph—out of
context. We cannot extract it and focus entirely on
the victory without including the lines which refer to
our responsibilities in the battle, to pray, to sacrifice,
to endure purification and coming trials. Many of the
elements prophesied at Fatima have come to pass,
and some are yet to happen. For this reason, now
more than ever, we must take seriously the call to
pray the Rosary every day to obtain peace, spiritual
peace, for our troubled world.

We are called to pray *from the heart*, from the
depths of the soul. Because we are united to the Mystical Body of Christ this prayer naturally and super-
naturally unites us to the suffering of the Body. We

will at times feel the very pain which is experienced in the Heart of our loving Jesus. Though He is the ascended and resurrected Lord, He is at the same time the Head and wholly united with His Mystical Body, including its members on earth. The Church is suffering on many levels, not only from exterior attacks, but also from the sins and disloyalty of its members, and all of this is mystically experienced by the Head of the Body.

The following meditation is worthy of our pondering as spiritual food for the contemporary call which lies before us to "make up what is lacking in the sufferings of Christ, for the sake of his body which is the Church" (Col 1:24):

> "His pain is beyond imagination. So many consecrated ones are piercing His Heart. So much duplicity in the world. The Pope is under extreme persecution. Satan is causing the ruin of a multitude of souls, but more people are responding to our Blessed Mother's call. Many souls have been saved today, but many more have perished. We must continue to pray for conversion and reparation. The Church will be given a tremendous trial soon. There will be great crisis in the faith the likes of which has never been seen before. In order to remain steadfast, we must look to Our Mother and pray her Rosary,

for she will crush the head of Satan but he will have caused much ruin. We are near the end of the time of Our Lord's Mercy. Those who don't believe will soon no longer be able to convert. Now is the time to act. We must die to ourselves in order to let the Lord reign in our hearts. We no longer have the luxury of time. We must offer ourselves up as living prayers to the Sacred Heart of Jesus and the Immaculate Heart of Mary.

"All that we do and say and pray must be offered up to the two Hearts. If we do this, we will be protected by their most precious hearts, but we must rest in their hearts in complete and total trust. The evil one will do anything and everything to try to wrestle us from the hearts of Jesus and Mary, but in the end, the Immaculate Heart of Mary will triumph and lead us to the reign of the Sacred Heart of Jesus and the Immaculate Heart of Mary. We must keep our minds, hearts, and souls singularly focused on the two hearts; if we do this, no one can distract us, even upon the pain of death. Our hearts will not falter if the eyes of our souls are focused on the glory of the Sacred Heart and the Immaculate Heart. We must not give into fear when all the world around us seems

> to collapse and the world does not re-
> semble what it is today.
> "Pray for those who do not believe, for
> those who do frivolous things, following
> the desires and passions of their own
> hearts. When the darkness comes, focus
> on the light of the Sacred Heart, which
> burns eternally in your soul. He is our light
> and salvation. Do not listen to the screams
> of the world, but only to the voice of Jesus
> speaking in the innermost chambers of our
> souls. Take heart, trust, and be still."

Sacred scripture prophetically refers to events of
"spiritual darkness" on several occasions: in Jeremiah,
"I looked on the earth, and lo, it was waste and void;
and to the heavens, and they had no light. I looked
on the mountains, and lo, they were quaking, and all
the hills moved to and fro. I looked, and lo, there was
no man, and all the birds of the air had fled. I looked,
and lo, the fruitful land was a desert, and all its cities
were laid in ruins before the Lord, before his fierce
anger" (Jer 4:23-27).

And from Exodus: "Then Yahweh said to Moses,
'Stretch out your hand toward Heaven, and let darkness, darkness so thick that it can be felt, cover the
land of Egypt.' So Moses stretched out his hand toward Heaven, and for three days there was deep
darkness over the whole land of Egypt. No one could
see anyone else or move about for three days, but

where the sons of Israel lived there was light for them" (Ex 10:21-23).

In the Gospel of St. Matthew, our Lord Himself describes an approaching time of darkness: "Immediately after the distress of those days, the sun will be darkened, the moon will lose its brightness, the stars will fall from the sky, and the powers of Heaven will be shaken" (Mt 24:29).

And yet clearly, a disciple of Christ should *never feel hopelessness or despair* when reading these passages. Remember that Jesus Himself tells us in the Gospel that, "When you see all these things happening, lift up your heads, because your redemption is near at hand" (Lk 21:27). To these scriptural prophesies must be added the words of our Holy Father: "There is no darkness so great that man must lose himself in it." God does not wish us to experience darkness, nor to perish. It is He who has offered us the light of mercy through His Son Jesus. Even in the very messages of Fatima and Akita, which speak of these upcoming purifications and darkness, that our Mother accentuates the imperative for us to be filled with hope, trust, and perseverance.

As a final examination of conscience, each of us must ask himself this question: "Am I attached to anything at all keeping me from compliance with our Mother's call to pray and work for the Dogma and the Triumph? Am I attached to any title, agenda, desire for personal advancement, even ecclesial advancement, any comfort, possession or power that stands in the way of complete union with the Sacred and Immaculate Hearts of Jesus and Mary, and in the way of complete submission to Pope John Paul II?" If so, let us immerse ourselves in the Divine Mercy of Jesus Christ. Let us flee to the confessional and be healed by He whom St. Augustine calls, the "Divine Physician." Let us fill our souls with the sublime graces that come only from daily Eucharistic reception and Adoration. Let the Rosary be our constant companion and spiritual weapon. Let us also pray the Chaplet of Divine Mercy to purify our hearts from anything which would restrict the flow of grace, resulting in the loss of faith, hope and love.

Could not the Loving Heart of Jesus say to each one of us:

> "You see the storm clouds gathering, my child; you recognize the signs of the times, and you feel the need deep inside your soul to draw near to Me in the shelter of My Heart. I have called you and you have heard Me and answered My call, but so many of My children do not hear Me, or have heard Me but do not heed Me or answer My call. O how My Heart weeps for them, My proud and willful children. They know the signs of the times, but they are too proud and afraid to recognize them. Their pride and willfulness keeps

them apart from Me, not by My choice, but by their own.

"The moment they would open their hearts and see the errors of their ways, they would fall immediately into the Mercy and shelter of My Heart, which waits for them.

"Pray for them, My child, so many of My children who do not rest in the love and mercy of My Heart. Pray as you have never prayed before, for the hour soon approaches.

"Stay close, My child, do not fear, I am with you always. Tell those who will listen to you to draw near to My Heart and fear nothing, for Your Jesus is the infinite source of Love and Mercy.

"Prepare your hearts, My Children. Do not let one moment pass between your heart and Mine. Rest in the shelter of My Heart and fear nothing, for those who stay small and humble, trusting in My Love and Mercy will remain hidden and protected in the chambers of My Heart.

"Many storms may howl around you, but they shall not consume you, My children, as long as your eyes remain focused on Me and not upon the turmoil that surrounds you.

"Keep the eyes of your soul, and the heart of your soul, focused continually upon Me, and I shall grant you peace in the midst of the greatest storm.

"Remember always, you are My precious children, and I am Your Jesus, Your Eucharistic Lord, the source of all love and mercy."

Yes, great storms may be approaching, and we may soon face great obstacles to the work of *Vox Populi* and all consecrated hearts dedicated to the Triumph of the Immaculate Heart. Let us be encouraged by the example of Saint Louis Marie de Montfort, who faced many obstacles in spreading true devotion to Mary. At one point, close to the end of his life, it appeared that he had failed. He had very few followers for the religious order he was called to found, and for the Marian spirituality of consecration he was called to spread. There was a temptation to discouragement and despair. On a journey, he saw a great valley, and he and the brother who accompanied him stopped to look at it. The brother gave voice to the temptation, saying, "Father de Montfort, are you sure that we have not strayed from the call?" Saint Louis replied, "My son, you see this great valley? In the future times it will be filled with souls consecrated to the Virgin Mother of God based on the consecration we spread."

We too must have this kind of faith. Every day we must renew our consecration to our Blessed Mother, who is forever Coredemptrix, Mediatrix, Advocate, through the consecration of St. Louis Marie de Montfort. In doing so we will renew our *fiat* , we will be strengthened to take whatever action our Lady asks of us for the sake of the Dogma and the Triumph. Let us truly obey, brothers and sisters in the Immaculate Heart, the exhortation of Sacred Scripture and our Holy Father, to "be not afraid." I encourage you and I ask you to join with me now with this renewal of Marian consecration so we all can be Totus Tuus people at the service of our Totus Tuus Pope, offering all that we are and all that we do for the Dogma, for the Triumph of the Immaculate Heart of Mary, or as co-redeemers with our Lady Coredemptrix in bringing to fruition the Eucharistic Reign of our Lord's Most Sacred Heart:

I, (Name), a faithless sinner, renew and ratify today in thy hands the vows of my Baptism; I renounce forever Satan, his pomps and works; and I give myself entirely to Jesus Christ, the Incarnate Wisdom, to carry my cross after Him all the days of my life, and to be more faithful to Him than I have ever been before.

In the presence of all the heavenly court I choose thee this day for my Mother and Mistress. I deliver and consecrate to thee, as thy slave, my body and soul, my goods, both interior and exterior, and even the value of all of my good actions, past, present, and future; leaving to thee the full right of disposing of me, and all that belongs to me, without exception, according to thy good pleasure, for the greater glory of God, in time and in eternity. Amen.

Appendix I:

Vox Populi Mariae Mediatrici Special Notification

Response to a Statement of an International Theological Commission of the Pontifical International Marian Academy
June 13, 1997

On 4 June 1997, a statement of a Theological Commission of the Pontifical International Marian Academy was published in *L'Osservatore Romano*. This commission was "asked by the Holy See to study the possibility and the opportuneness of a definition of the Marian titles of Mediatrix, Coredemptrix and Advocate." The commission was composed of fifteen Catholic theologians and additional non-Catholic theologians, including an Anglican, a Lutheran and three Orthodox theologians.

Although I wish to express my appreciation for the furthering of the theological dialogue regarding the solemn definition of the Maternal Mediation of the Blessed Virgin Mary as provided by this statement of the international theological commission, I must at the same time state that there are several theological elements foundational to this question that appear to be missing from the considerations and conclusions of the commission. I will summarize only the more critical theological elements absent from the statement and conclusions of the commission, theological elements which are contained in the work of another international association of theologians and mariologists who have contributed to the two theological volumes dedicated to the question of the Maternal Mediation of Mary: *Mary Coredemptrix, Mediatrix, Advocate: Theological Foundations, Towards A Papal Definition?*, and *Mary Coredemptrix, Mediatrix, Advocate: Theological Foundations II, Papal, Pneumatological, Ecumenical* (Queenship Publishing, Santa Barbara, CA). The internationally respected theologians who participated in this serious theological study pertinent to the question of the solemn definition of the Maternal Mediation of Mary span several continents, many countries, and three communities of Christianity.

1. The Title, "Coredemptrix" and the Papal Teachings of Pope John Paul II

A primary caution seems to be against the specific use of the title "Coredemptrix" in discussing the unique cooperation of the Blessed Virgin Mary with and under Jesus Christ in the Redemption of humanity. *It must be strongly underscored that our present Holy Father, Pope John Paul II, has used the explicit title "Coredemptrix" on at least five occasions in Papal Teach-*

ings during his present pontificate.[1] This is well illustrated in the 1985 Papal Address of Pope John Paul II in Guayaquil, Ecuador, where both the title "Coredemptrix" is used and an explanation of the role is given:

> "Mary goes before us and accompanies us. The silent journey that begins with her Immaculate Conception and passes through the 'yes' of Nazareth, which makes her the Mother of God, finds on Calvary a particularly important moment. There also, accepting and assisting at the sacrifice of her son, Mary is the dawn of Redemption;...Crucified spiritually with her crucified son (cf. Gal. 2:20), she contemplated with heroic love the death of her God, she "lovingly consented to the immolation of this Victim which she herself had brought forth" (*Lumen Gentium*, 58)...
>
> "In fact, at Calvary she united herself with the sacrifice of her Son that led to the foundation of the Church; her maternal heart shared to the very depths the will of Christ 'to gather into one all the dispersed children of God' (Jn. 11:52). Having suffered for the Church, Mary deserved to become the Mother of all the disciples of her Son, the Mother of their unity....In fact,

Mary's role as Coredemptrix did not cease with the glorification of her Son"[2]

More recently, in his general audience address of 9 April 1997 (at present the Holy Father has given a series of over 50 Marian catecheses), the Holy Father uses the example of St. Paul's call for all Christians to be "God's fellow workers" (1 Cor. 3:9), or in some translations "co-workers," and also specifies Mary's unique co-operation in the work of redemption (without inferring any equality between Christians, the Blessed Virgin Mary, and the unique act of redemption accomplished by Jesus Christ alone):

> "Moreover, when the Apostle Paul says: "For we are God's fellow workers" (1 Cor 3:9), he maintains the real possibility for man to co-operate with God. The collaboration of believers, which obviously excludes any equality with him, is expressed in the proclamation of the Gospel and in their personal contribution to its taking root in human hearts.
>
> "However, applied to Mary, the term 'co-operator' acquires a specific meaning. The collaboration of Christians in salvation takes place after the Calvary event, whose fruits they endeavor to spread by prayer and sacrifice. Mary, instead, co-operated during the event itself and in the

role of mother; thus her co-operation embraces the whole of Christ's saving work. She alone was associated in this way with the redemptive sacrifice that merited the salvation of all mankind. In union with the Christ and in submission to him, she collaborated in obtaining the grace of salvation for all humanity."[3]

In all instances of papal usuage of the term, "Coredemptrix," the prefix "co" does not mean "equal to" but comes from the Latin word, *"cum"* which means "with." *The title of "Coredemptrix" applied to the Mother of Jesus never places Mary on a level of equality with Jesus Christ, the divine Lord of all, in the saving process of humanity's redemption.* Rather, it denotes Mary's singular and unique sharing with her Son in the saving work of redemption for the human family. The Mother of Jesus participates in the redemptive work of her Saviour Son, who alone could reconcile humanity with the Father in his glorious divinity and humanity.[4]

Hence the title and role of Mary as Coredemptrix reveals Mary's unique participation, her "co-working" and "co-operating" with and under Jesus Christ, the sole Redeemer of humanity, while at the same time calling all Christians to cooperate in the saving work of redemption (cf. Col. 1:24). The teaching of our Holy Father that "the collaboration of believers... obviously excludes any equality with him..." corrects the somewhat misleading statement made in a commentary to the statement of the theological commission that the title "Coredemptrix" or the doctrine of Marian coredemption inappropriately "names" Mary as a mere creature to be "on the level with the Word of God in his particular redemptive function." Moreover, *Lumen Gentium*, n. 62 clarifies the rightful participation of creatures in the one mediation of Jesus Christ without the confusion of being inappropriately perceived as being on "the level with the Word of God":

> "No creature could ever be counted along with the Incarnate Word and Redeemer; but just as the priesthood of Christ is shared in various ways both by his ministers and the faithful, and as the one goodness of God is radiated in different ways among his creatures, so also the unique mediation of the Redeemer does not exclude but rather gives rise to a manifold cooperation which is but a sharing in this one source" (*Lumen Gentium*, n. 62).

No claim is made here that the documents of the present Holy Father, where he employs the title "Coredemptrix," are the most definitive of his pontificate, as has been alluded to by commentators of the commission. At the same time, it would constitute an even greater error to unjustifiably claim that the Papal Teachings of John Paul II and the explicit usage of the title "Coredemptrix" have no theological importance and significance. They are clear, repeated, indications of how the Holy Father understands and would define what makes the Virgin Mother's cooperation in the work of redemption under the Cross singular and non-repeatable by any other believer. To say that her cooperation is singular is not to say it is equal to Christ's work. And to specifically designate this unique participation of Mary, the "New Eve," with and under Jesus Christ, the "New Adam," as *Marian Coredemption*," so as to *define* the singularity of that cooperation, hardly seems imprecise and ambiguous—anymore than it would be imprecise or ambiguous to the divine primacy of Jesus Christ to define the singular cooperation of the Blessed Virgin in the Incarnation of Jesus Christ as Mother of God.

The further objection that "the titles as proposed are ambiguous" must be seen, again, in light of the rich Papal Magisterial Teaching of the nineteenth and twentieth centuries. Not only was the term "Coredemptrix" used under the pontificates of Pius X and Pius XI along with its contemporary usage by the present Holy Father, but the subsequent terms "Mediatrix" and "Advocate" have an even greater frequency of usage and teaching by the nineteenth and twentieth century Papal Magisterium.[5] Not only are the terms "Mediatrix" and "Advocate" contained in the teachings of the Second Vatican Council (cf.

Lumen Gentium, n.62), but they are developed in great measure in the 1987 Papal Encyclical, *Redemptoris Mater* (Mother of the Redeemer), with the entire third section entitled and dedicated to the Church doctrine of "Maternal Mediation."[6] Perhaps the "ambiguity" mentioned by the theological commission came from a lack of full understanding that the object of the petition is a solemn definition of the Maternal Mediation of Mary under its three essential aspects of Coredemptrix ("the Mother Suffering"), Mediatrix ("the Mother Nourishing"), and Advocate ("the Mother Interceding"), and not a request for a "triple dogma" or "three non-homogeneous terms" as members of the commission have previously stated. The roles of a mother, as heart of the family, are multiformed; the truth of her motherhood is singular. The same holds true for the "Mother of the Church" (cf. Second Vatican Council, Nov. 21, 1964).

2. The Solemn Definition of Maternal Mediation and the Second Vatican Council

It must also be remembered that the Second Vatican Council was by its own self-definition not a "dogmatic council" but a "pastoral council," and as such may not have been the most appropriate setting for a dogmatic definition. And yet, the Council Fathers made it clear that they did not intend to present a "complete doctrine on Mary" and encouraged future mariological doctrinal development:

"This sacred synod...does not, however, intend to give a complete doctrine on Mary, nor does it wish to decide those questions which the work of theologians has not yet fully clarified" (*Lumen Gentium*, n. 52). Church history and precedence teaches us that the decision of a given ecumenical council not to make a solemn definition does not preclude a solemn definition coming in an *ex cathedra* fashion in the future. For example, a petition for the solemn definition of the Assumption of Mary was raised and rejected at Vatican Council I, but this did not prevent the later solemn definition of the Assumption by Pius XII in an *ex cathedra* expression. There are no grounds for concluding that because Vatican II abstained from using the title "Coredemptrix," that therefore the Council intended the Church to abandon the use of this title forever. The mariological doctrine, language, and usage of the title by Pope John Paul II clearly make any such conclusion impossible.

For this and for many other reasons, therefore, the rich mariological doctrinal development on the subject of Mary's Maternal Mediation provided by the Papal Teachings of John Paul II is a fruitful development of the teaching of the Second Vatican Council offered. We must be aware of any mode of theological stagnancy that would reject authentic mariological doctrinal development as manifested by the present Pontiff in his Papal Magisterium, both in expressions of encyclicals, apostolic letters, and general papal addresses and teachings.

3. The Solemn Definition of Maternal Mediation and Ecumenism

Regarding sensitivity to "ecumenical difficulties" expressed by the theological commission, let us again return to the clear teaching of Pope John Paul II, a contemporary prophet for the critical call of Ecumenism in his recent encyclical on Ecumenism, *Ut Unum Sint*. Within this papal instruction on the ecclesial mandate for authentic ecumenical activity, John Paul II specifies that in our efforts of authentic Catholic Ecumenism, the whole body of doctrine as taught by the Church must be presented; full communion in the one body of Christ can only take place through the acceptance of the whole truth as taught by the Church, and that the "demands of revealed truth" does not prevent ecumenical activity, but rather provides the necessary foundation for ultimate union. *Ut Unum Sint* states:

> "With regard to the study of areas of disagreement, the Council requires that the whole body of doctrine be clearly presented... Full communion of course will have to come about through the acceptance of the whole truth into which the Holy Spirit guides Christ's disciples. Hence all forms of reductionism or facile "agreement" must be absolutely avoided[7]... unity willed by God can be at-

tained only by the adherence of all to the content of revealed faith in its entirety. In matters of faith, compromise is in contradiction with God who is Truth. In the Body of Christ, 'the way, and the truth, and the life' (Jn 14:6), who could consider legitimate a reconciliation brought about at the expense of the truth?[8]....To uphold a vision of unity which takes account of all the demands of revealed truth does not mean to put a brake on the ecumenical movement.[9] On the contrary, it means preventing it from settling for apparent solutions which would lead to no firm and solid results. The obligation to respect the truth is absolute. Is this not the law of the Gospel?"[10]

In that same document on Ecumenism, the Holy Father defends the exercise of the charism of papal infallibility as a "witness to the truth" which in fact serves as a value and foundation for ultimate Christian unity:

"When circumstances require it, [the Pope] speaks in the name of all the Pastors in communion with him. He can also—under very specific conditions clearly laid down by the First Vatican Council—declare *ex cathedra* that a certain doctrine belongs to the deposit of faith

> (First Vatican Ecumenical Council, *Pastor Aeternus*: *DS* 3074). By thus bearing witness to the truth, he serves unity."[11]

Solemn definitions of Marian dogmas, and in specific the solemn definition of Maternal Mediation, does not run counter to the Church's critical mandate of ecumenical activity; rather such definitions can serve this unity for the sake of doctrinal perfection and clarity, as we find in the words of John Cardinal O'Connor of New York: "Clearly, a formal definition would be articulated in such precise terminology that other Christians would lose their anxiety that we do not distinguish adequately between Mary's unique association with the redemption and the redemptive power exercised by Christ alone."[12]

At the same time we should not be surprised when Christian brothers and sisters from other communions who do not accept the office and charism of the papacy are not in favor of the exercise of the very office which they themselves do not accept as authentic. Therefore to require convincing support from other Christians and ecclesial bodies as a requisite condition for the exercise of papal infallibility would, practically speaking, effectively eliminate this charism given by the Holy Spirit and Christ to the Church for the sake of doctrinal clarity and perfection.

The Blessed Virgin Mary must be seen not as the obstacle, but as the instrument and Mother of the ecumenical movement (cf. *Redemptoris Mater*, n. 30), remembering that no one unites the children of a family more than the mother of that family. Let us confidently leave such decisions of timeliness and opportuneness to the present Vicar of Christ, Pope John Paul II, who is at the same time both *fully Marian* and *fully ecumenical*.

4. *Vox Populi Mariae Mediatrici*

The international Catholic organization, *Vox Populi Mariae Mediatrici* (Voice of the People for Mary Mediatrix), is a principal movement amidst others petitioning our Holy Father, Pope John Paul II, to solemnly define the Maternal Mediation of the Blessed Virgin Mary. This international Catholic organization carries with it the episcopal endorsements of over 500 bishops, inclusive of 42 Cardinals and 4.5 million petitions from the faithful spanning over 155 countries, all united in the requesting of the solemn definition of Our Lady's Maternal Mediation. *Vox Populi Mariae Mediatrici works in complete obedience and solidarity to the Papal Magisterium of Pope John Paul II* in exercising the canonical right and duty encoded in Canon 212, §2,3:

> "The Christian faithful are free to make known their needs, especially spiritual ones, and their desires to the pastors of the Church"; "In accord with the knowl-

edge, competence and preeminence which they possess, they have the right and even at times a duty to manifest to the sacred pastors their opinion on matters which pertain to the good of the Church, and they have a right to make their opinion known to the other Christian faithful, with due regard for the integrity of faith and morals and reverence toward their pastors, and with consideration for the common good and the dignity of persons."

In the proper letter and spirit of this Canon, *Vox Populi Mariae Mediatrici* continues to do all possible on the level of prayer, theological research, Marian catechesis and education of the faithful to assist in bringing to proper theological and ecclesial maturity the cause of the solemn definition of the Maternal Mediation of the Blessed Virgin Mary.

In light of the objection of the commission that the mariological doctrine in question still needs "further study" and "theological maturity," let us recall from our recent past Church precedence that such maturity can come about in a rather brief span of time, based on the given minds and hearts, both authoritative and theological, dedicated to the development of a given doctrine at a given time of the Church. For example, in 1957 Pius XII stated that the cause of restoration of the permanent diaconate at that time lacked "theological maturity." It was only a very few years later at the Second Vatican Council (1961-1965) that the permanent diaconate was seen as "having reached" its "proper theological maturity," and hence was reinstated by Pope Paul VI shortly after the Council in 1967.

In sum then, this statement of the theological commission, while providing a valuable contribution to the theological dialogue concerning Maternal Mediation and its potential definition, neither constitutes nor contains any authoritative or official prohibition of the continued activities of *Vox Populi Mariae Mediatrici*, which will continue to work in obedience and solidarity to the Papal Magisterium of Pope John Paul II in seeking to bring about the necessary theological and ecclesial maturity for the solemn definition of Maternal Mediation, whether that be in the distant or "not too distant" future. The final and definitive judgment of which, of course, remains with the present Pontiff. And with all proper appreciation and respect for the contribution of the theological commission, we know from the historical precedence of the Church that several advisory theological commissions requested by the Holy See have come to conclusions which ultimately were not adopted by the Holy See; the most radical example within recent Church precedence having been the theological commission requested by the Holy See to examine the question of artificial birth control, the conclusion of which was overridden by Pope Paul VI when he reaffirmed the constant Church teaching against artificial birth control in his 1968 Encyclical, *Humanae Vitae*.[13]

IN CONCLUSION, THE FOLLOWING SUMMARY STATEMENTS CAN BE ARTICULATED:

1. The present Pontiff, Pope John Paul II has used the title "Coredemptrix" for the Blessed Virgin Mary on at least five occasions in Papal statements accompanied by a profound teaching on the unique participation of the Blessed Virgin Mary in the redemption of humanity by Jesus Christ. The titles and roles of "Mediatrix" and "Advocate" are contained in the teachings of the Second Vatican Council (*Lumen Gentium*, n. 8) and have a rich tradition and usage in the Papal Magisterium of the nineteenth and twentieth centuries (with special contribution by the present Papal Magisterium of John Paul II).

2. The teachings of the Second Vatican Council in no way prohibit a solemn definition on Maternal Mediation, and in fact call for a proper theological development and completion of authentic Marian doctrine (cf. *Lumen Gentium*, n. 54).

3. The specific contribution found in the Papal Teachings of Pope John Paul II on the subject of the Maternal Mediation of Mary as Coredemptrix, Mediatrix, and Advocate must be included and appreciated in the contemporary development of

mariological doctrine, potentially leading to a solemn definition of Maternal Mediation.

4. The request for a solemn definition of the Maternal Mediation of Mary in no way runs counter to the critical ecclesial mandate for authentic ecumenical activity. The "whole truth about Mary" as part of the "whole truth of the Gospel" will serve as the foundation for ultimate Christian unity, as taught by Christ and entrusted to the Church (cf. *Dei Verbum*, n. 9, 10). In the words of Pope John Paul II : "To uphold a vision of unity which takes account of all the demands of revealed truth does not mean to put a brake on the ecumenical movement."[14] The Blessed Virgin Mary must be seen not as an obstacle, but as a maternal instrument of unity of all Christians into the one fold of Jesus Christ.

5. The international Catholic movement, *Vox Populi Mariae Mediatrici,* constituting 500 bishops, 42 cardinals, and the petitions of 4.5 million faithful spanning 155 countries, will continue to pray and work in obedience to the Papal Magisterium of Pope John Paul II, in striving for the theological and ecclesial maturity required for the solemn definition of the Maternal Mediation of Mary as Coredemptrix, Mediatrix, and Advocate, as is its canonical right and duty expressed in Canon 212, §2,3.

6. *Vox Populi Mariae Mediatrici* leaves the ultimate discernment and decision of the "possibility and opportuneness" of the solemn definition of the Maternal Mediation of the Blessed Virgin Mary to

His Holiness Pope John Paul II, and offers full obedience and submission to his final and definitive judgment.

Dr. Mark I. Miravalle, S.T.D.
International President, *Vox Populi Mariae Mediatrici*
Professor of Theology and Mariology
Franciscan University of Steubenville

Notes

[1] In his greetings to the sick after the general audience of 8 September 1982 the Pope said: "Mary, though conceived and born without the taint of sin, participated in a marvelous way in the sufferings of her divine Son, in order to be *Coredemptrix of humanity*" (*Insegnamenti di Giovanni Paolo II, I* , V/3 (1982) 404);

In 1984 in his Angelus address in Arona: "To Our Lady—*the Coredemptrix*—St. Charles turned with singularly revealing accents" (*Inseg* VII/2 (1984) 1151 [*ORE* 860:1]);

On 31 January 1985, in an address at the Marian shrine in Guayaquil, Ecuador: "Mary goes before us and accompanies us. The silent journey that begins with her Immaculate Conception and passes through the 'yes' of Nazareth, which makes her the Mother of God, finds on Calvary a particularly important moment. There also, *accepting and assisting at the sacrifice of her son*, Mary is the dawn of Redemption;... *Crucified spiritually with her crucified son* (cf. Gal. 2:20), she contemplated with heroic love the death of her God, she "lovingly consented to the immolation of this Victim which she herself had brought forth" (*Lumen Gentium,* 58)...In fact, at Calvary *she united herself with the sacrifice of her Son that led to the foundation of the Church; her maternal heart shared to the very depths the will of Christ 'to gather into one all the dispersed children of God'* (Jn.

11:52). *Having suffered for the Church*, Mary deserved to become the Mother of all the disciples of her Son, the Mother of their unity....The Gospels do not tell us of an appearance of the risen Christ to Mary. Nevertheless, as she was in a special way close to the Cross of her Son, she also had to have a privileged experience of his Resurrection. In fact, *Mary's role as Coredemptrix* did not cease with the glorification of her Son" (*Inseg* VIII / 1 (1985) 318-319 [*ORE* 876:7]);

On 31 March 1985, Palm Sunday and World Youth Day: "At the Angelus hour on this Palm Sunday, which the Liturgy calls also the Sunday of the Lord's Passion, our thoughts run to Mary, immersed in the mystery of an immeasurable sorrow. Mary accompanied her divine Son in the most discreet concealment pondering everything in the depths of her heart. On Calvary, at the foot of the Cross, in the vastness and in the depth of her maternal sacrifice, she had John, the youngest Apostle, beside her....May, Mary our Protectress, *the Coredemptrix*, to whom we offer our prayer with great outpouring, make our desire generously correspond to the desire of the Redeemer" (*Inseg* VIII / 1 (1985) 889-890 [*ORE* 880:12]);

In commemorating the sixth centenary of the canonization of St. Bridget of Sweden on 6 October 1991: "Birgitta looked to Mary as her model and support in the various moments of her life. She spoke energetically about the divine privilege of Mary's Immaculate Conception. She contemplated her astonishing mission as Mother of the Saviour. She invoked her as the Immaculate Conception, Our Lady of Sorrows, and *Coredemptrix*, exalting Mary's singular role in the history of salvation and the life of the Christian people" (*Inseg* XIV/2 (1991) 756 [*ORE* 1211:4]. Cf. Monsignor Arthur Calkins, "John Paul II's Teaching on Marian Coredemption," as found in *Mary Coredemptrix, Mediatrix, Advocate: Theological Foundations II, Papal, Pneumatological, Ecumenical*, 1997, Queenship Publishing, Santa Barbara, CA.

2   Cf. Miravalle, *Mary Coredemptrix, Mediatrix, Advocate: Theological Foundations, Towards A Papal Definition?*, 1995, Queenship Publishing, Santa Barbara, CA.

3   Pope John Paul II, General Audience of 9 April, *L'Osservatore Romano*, p. 7, 16 April English ed.

4   See Miravalle, "Mary Coredemptrix, Mediatrix, Advocate: Foundational Presence in Divine Revelation" as found in *Mary Coredemptrix, Mediatrix, Advocate: Theological Foundations, Towards A Papal Definition*, 1995, Queenship Publishing, Santa Barbara, CA.

5   Cf. Rev. John Schug, "Mary, Coredemptrix: The Significance of her Title in the Magisterium of The Church" as found in *Mary Coredemptrix, Mediatrix, Advocate: Theological Foundations, Towards A Papal Definition*, 1995, Queenship Publishing, Santa Barbara, CA; and Monsignor Arthur Calkins, "John

Paul II's Teaching on Marian Coredemption," as found in *Mary Coredemptrix, Mediatrix, Advocate: Theological Foundations II, Papal, Pneumatological, Ecumenical*, 1997, Queenship Publishing, Santa Barbara, CA.

6   Pope John Paul II, *Redemptoris Mater*, n.3.

7   Pope John Paul II, *Ut Unum Sint*, n.36.

8   *Ibid*, n.18.

9   Cf. Address to the Cardinals and Roman Curia (June 28, 1985),6:*AAS* 77 (1985), 1153; cf. *Ut Unum Sint*, n.79.

10   *Ut Unum Sint*, n.79.

11   *Ut Unum Sint*, n.94.

12   John Cardinal O'Connor, Letter of Endorsement to *Vox Populi Mariae Mediatrici*, Feb. 14, 1994, as published in *Mary Coredemptrix, Mediatrix, Advocate, Cardinal Endorsements*, Queenship Publications, Santa Barbara, CA.,1994.

13   Pope Paul VI, Encyclical Letter, *Humanae Vitae*, 1968, p. 6, n.6, Daughters of St. Paul, Boston, MA.

14   Cf. Address to the Cardinals and Roman Curia (June 28, 1985),6:*AAS* 77 (1985), 1153; cf. *Ut Unum Sint*, n.79.

Clarification Regarding Statement of Vatican Spokesman Joaquin Navarro-Valls, 18 August 1997

Many conflicting reports from the media surfaced in response to the August 18 statement of Vatican spokesman Joaquin Navarro-Valls regarding the potential papal definition of Mary as Coredemptrix, Mediatrix, and Advocate. The interest of the media was due to the August 25 *Newsweek* cover story on the subject.

Although no written statement has been produced from the Vatican office, the oral statement received from the office of Joaquin Navarro-Valls was as follows:

> "This [the dogma] is not presently under study by any Vatican congregation or commission."

This statement *in no way precludes a papal definition by the Holy Father* in the exercise of papal infallibility. Various news reports have gone to such excesses as to say that the Pope will not or will never proclaim this dogma. Those reports are neither part of nor representative of the official position of the Vatican.

Vox Populi Mariae Mediatrici continues its work at the service of the Church in conformity with canon 212 of the Code of Canon Law:

> "The Christian faithful are free to make known their needs, especially spiritual ones, and their desires to the pastors of the Church"; "In accord with the knowledge, competence and preeminence which they possess, they have the right and even at times a duty to manifest to the sacred pastors their opinion on matters which pertain to the good of the Church, and they have a right to make their opinion known to the other Christian faithful, with due regard for the integrity of faith and morals and reverence toward their pastors, and with consideration for the common good and the dignity of persons."

Vox Populi Mariae Mediatrici

Appendix III:

Recent Papal Audiences on Marian Coredemption, Mediation, and Advocacy

The following Wednesday audiences by our Holy Father, Pope John Paul II on 2 April 1997 (entitled "Mary United Herself to Jesus' Offering"), 9 April 1997 ("Mary's Co-operation Is Totally Unique"), 24 September 1997 ("Mary Has Universal Spiritual Motherhood")and 1 October 1997 ("Mary, Mediatrix") have been included in this appendix because of their immediate relevance to the subject of the Maternal Mediation of Our Lady. Intrinsic to the 24 September and 1 October audiences are answers to many of the objections posed by the Theological Commission (*L'Osservatore Romano*, 4 June 1997) regarding the doctrinal teaching of Maternal Mediation.

N.15   **L'OSSERVATORE ROMANO**   **Weekly Edition 11**

Mary united herself to Jesus' offering

By consenting to her Son's sacrifice, the Blessed Virgin had a part in his self-offering to the Father as the victim who takes away the world's sins

"With our gaze illumined by the radiance of the Resurrection, we pause to reflect on the Mother's involvement in her Son's redeeming Passion, which was completed by her sharing in his suffering," the Holy Father said at the General Audience of Wednesday, 2 April 1997, as he reflected on Mary's participation in the mystery of Redemption and her presence at the foot of the Cross. Here is a translation of his catechesis, which was given in Italian.

1. *Regina caeli laetare, alleluia!*

So the Church sings in this Easter season, inviting the faithful to join in the spiritual joy of Mary, Mother of the Redeemer. The Blessed Virgin's gladness at Christ's Resurrection is even greater if one considers her intimate participation in Jesus' entire life.

In accepting with complete availability the words of the Angel Gabriel, who announced to her that she would become the Mother of the Messiah, Mary began her participation in the drama of Redemption. Her involvement in her Son's sacrifice, revealed by Simeon during the presentation in the Temple, continues not only in the episode of the losing and finding of the 12-year-old Jesus, but also throughout his public life.

However, the Blessed Virgin's association with Christ's mission reaches its culmination in Jerusalem, at the time of the Redeemer's Passion and Death. As the Fourth Gospel testifies, she was in the Holy City at the time, probably for the celebration of the Jewish feast of Passover.

2. The Council stresses the profound dimension of the Blessed Virgin's presence on Calvary, recalling that she "faithfully persevered in her union with her Son unto the Cross" (*Lumen gentium*, n.58), and points out that this union "in the work of salvation is made manifest from the time of Christ's virginal conception up to his death" (ibid., n.57).

Mary joins her suffering to Jesus' priestly sacrifice

With our gaze illumined by the radiance of the Resurrection, we pause to reflect on the Mother's involvement in her Son's redeeming Passion, which was completed by her sharing in his suffering. Let us return again, but now in the perspective of the Resurrection, to the foot of the Cross where the Mother endured "with her only-begotten Son the intensity of his suffering, associated herself with his sacrifice in her mother's heart, and lovingly consented to the immolation of this victim which was born of her" (ibid., n.58).

With these words, the Council reminds us of "Mary's compassion"; in her heart reverberates all that Jesus suffers in body and soul, emphasizing her willingness to share in her Son's redeeming sacrifice and to join her own maternal suffering to his priestly offering.

The Council text also stresses that her consent to Jesus' immolation is not passive acceptance but a genuine act of love, by which she offers her Son as a "victim" of expiation for the sins of all humanity.

Lastly, *Lumen gentium* relates the Blessed Virgin to Christ, who has the lead role in Redemption, making it clear that in associating herself "with his sacrifice' she remains subordinate to her divine Son.

3. In the Fourth Gospel, St. John says that "standing by the Cross of Jesus were his mother, and his mother's sister, Mary the wife of Clopas, and Mary Magdalene" (19:25). By using the verb "to stand," which literally means "to be on one's feet," "to stand erect," perhaps the Evangelist intends to present the dignity and strength shown in their sorrow by Mary and the other women.

The Blessed Virgin's "standing erect" at the foot of the Cross recalls her unfailing constancy and extraordinary courage in facing suffering. In the tragic events of Calvary, Mary is sustained by faith, strengthened during the events of her life and especially during Jesus' public life. The Council recalls that "the Blessed Virgin advanced in her pilgrimage of faith and faithfully persevered in her union with her Son unto the Cross" (*Lumen gentium*, n.58).

Sharing his deepest feelings, she counters the arrogant insults addressed to the crucified Messiah with forbearance and pardon, associating herself with his prayer to the Father: "Forgive them, for they know not what they do" (Lk 23:34). By sharing in the feeling of abandonment to the Father's will expressed in Jesus' last words on the Cross: "Father into your hands I commend my spirit!" (ibid., 23:46), she thus offers, as the Council notes, loving consent "to the immolation of this victim which was born of her" (*Lumen gentium*, n.58).

Mary's hope contains light stronger than darkness

4. Mary's supreme "yes" is radiant with trusting hope in the mysterious future, begun with the death of her crucified Son. The words in which Jesus taught the disciples on his way to Jerusalem "that the Son of man must suffer many things, and be rejected by the elders and the chief priests and the scribes, and be killed, and after three days rise again" re-echo in her heart at the dramatic hour of Calvary, awakening expectation of and yearning for the Resurrection.

Mary's hope at the foot of the Cross contains a light stronger than the darkness that reigns in many hearts: in the presence of the redeeming Sacrifice, the hope of the Church and of humanity is born in Mary.

Reprinted from *L'Osservatore Romano*, English Edition.

N.16   L'OSSERVATORE ROMANO   Weekly Edition 7

Mary's co-operation is totally unique

The basis of this singular co-operation is Mary's divine motherhood and her sharing in Jesus' life, culminating in her presence at the foot of the Cross.

"We can... turn to the Blessed Virgin, trustfully imploring her aid in the awareness of the singular role entrusted to her by God, the role of co-operator in the Redemption, which she exercised throughout her life and in a special way at the foot of the Cross," the Holy Father said at the General Audience of Wednesday, 9 April 1997. The Pope was continuing his catechesis on the role of the Blessed Mother, calling attention to her unique co-operation in the work of salvation. Here is a translation of his reflection, which was the 48th in the series on the Blessed Virgin and was given in Italian.

1. Down the centuries the Church has reflected on Mary's co-operation in the work of salvation, deepening the analysis of her association with Christ's redemptive sacrifice. St. Augustine already gave the Blessed Virgin the title "co-operator" in the Redemption (cf. *De Sancta Virginitate*, 6; *PL* 40, 399), a title which emphasizes Mary's joint but subordinate action with Christ the Redeemer.

Reflection has developed along these lines, particularly since the 15th century. Some feared there might be a desire to put Mary on the same level as Christ. Actually the Church's teaching makes a clear distinction between the Mother and the Son in the work o salvation, explaining the Blessed Virgin's subordination, as co-operator, to the one Redeemer.

Moreover, when the Apostle Paul says: "For we are God's fellow workers" (1 Cor 3:9), he maintains the real possibility for man to co-operate with God.

The collaboration of believers, which obviously excludes any equality with him, is expressed in the proclamation of the Gospel and in their personal contribution to its taking root in human hearts.

Mary's co-operation is unique and unrepeatable

2. However, applied to Mary, the term "co-operator" acquires a specific meaning. The collaboration of Christians in salvation takes place after the Calvary event, whose fruits they endeavor to spread by prayer and sacrifice. Mary, instead, co-operated during the event itself and in the role of mother; thus her co-operation embraces the whole of Christ's saving work. She alone was associated in this way with the redemptive sacrifice that merited the salvation of all mankind. In union with Christ and in submission to him, she collaborated in obtaining the grace of salvation for all humanity.

The Blessed Virgin's role as co-operator has its source in her divine motherhood. By giving birth to the One who was destined to achieve man's redemption, by nourishing him, presenting him in the temple and suffering with him as he died on the Cross, "in a wholly singular way she co-operated...in the work of the Saviour" (*Lumen gentium*, n.61). Although God's call to co-operate in the work of salvation concerns every human being, the participation of the Saviour's Mother in humanity's Redemption is a unique and unrepeatable fact.

Despite the uniqueness of her condition, Mary is also the recipient of salvation. She is the first to be saved, redeemed by Christ "in the most sublime way" in her Immaculate Conception (cf. Bull *Ineffabilis Deus*, in Pius IX, *Acta*, 1, 605) and filled with the grace of the Holy Spirit.

3. This assertion now leads to the question: what is the meaning of Mary's unique co-operation in the plan of salvation? It should be sought in God's particular intention for the Mother of the Redeemer, whom on two solemn occasions, that is, at Cana and beneath the Cross, Jesus addresses as "Woman" (cf. Jn 2,4; 19:26). Mary is associated as a woman in the work of salvation. Having created man "male and female" (cf. Gen 1:27), the Lord also wants to place the New Eve beside the New Adam in the Redemption. Our first parents had chosen the way of sin as a couple; a new pair, the Son of God with his Mother's co-operation, would re-establish the human race in its original dignity.

Mary, the New Eve, thus becomes a perfect icon of the Church. In the divine plan, at the foot of the Cross, she represents redeemed humanity which, in need of salvation, is enabled to make a contribution to the unfolding of the saving work.

Mary is our mother in the order of grace

4. The Council had this doctrine in mind and made it its own, stressing the Blessed Virgin's contri-

bution not only to the Redeemer's birth, but also to the life of his Mystical Body down the ages until the "eschaton": in the Church Mary has "co-operated" (cf. *Lumen gentium*, n. 63) and "co-operates" (cf. ibid., n.53) in the work of salvation. In describing the mystery of the Annunciation, the Council states that the Virgin of Nazareth, "committing herself wholeheartedly and impeded by no sin to God's saving will, devoted herself totally, as a handmaid of the Lord, to the person and work of her Son, under and with him, serving the mystery of Redemption by the grace of Almighty God" (ibid., n.56).

The Second Vatican Council moreover presents Mary not only as "Mother of the divine Redeemer," but also " in a singular way [as] the generous associate," who "co-operated by her obedience, faith, hope and burning charity in the work of the Saviour." The Council also recalls that the sublime fruit of this co-operation is her universal motherhood: "For this reason she is a mother to us in the order of grace" (ibid., n.61).

We can therefore turn to the Blessed Virgin, trustfully imploring her aid in the awareness of the singular role entrusted to her by God, the role of co-operator in the Redemption, which she exercised throughout her life and in a special way at the foot of the Cross.

Reprinted from *L'Osservatore Romano*, English Edition.

Mary has universal spiritual motherhood

Our Lady is mother of all humanity because she co-operated with faith, hope and charity in Christ's work of restoring supernatural life to souls.

The Blessed Virgin, "having entered the Father's eternal kingdom, closer to her divine Son and thus closer to us all, can more effectively exercise in the Spirit the role of maternal intercession entrusted to her by divine Providence," the Holy Father said at the General Audience of Wednesday, 24 September, as he discussed Mary's motherhood in the order of grace. He went on to explain the meaning of the Marian titles of Advocate, Helper, Benefactress and Mediatrix. Here is a translation of the Pope's catechesis, which was the 64th in the series on the Blessed Virgin and was given in Italian.

1. Mary is mother of humanity in the order of grace. The Second Vatican Council highlights this role of Mary, linking it to her co-operation in Christ's Redemption.

"In the designs of divine Providence, she was the gracious mother of the divine Redeemer here on earth, and above all others and in a singular way the generous associate and humble handmaid of the Lord" (*Lumen gentium*, n.61).

With these statements, the Constitution *Lumen gentium* wishes to give proper emphasis to the fact that the Blessed Virgin was intimately associated with Christ's redemptive work, becoming the Saviour's "generous associate," "in a singular way."

With the actions of any mother, from the most ordinary to the most demanding, Mary freely co-operated in the work of humanity's salvation in profound and constant harmony with her divine Son.

Our Lady's motherhood has universal scope

2. The Council also points out that Mary's co-operation was inspired by the Gospel virtues of obedience, faith, hope and charity, and was accomplished under the influence of the Holy Spirit. It also recalls that the gift of her universal spiritual motherhood stems precisely from this co-operation; associated with Christ in the work of Redemption, which includes the spiritual regeneration of humanity, she becomes mother of those reborn to new life.

In saying that Mary is "a mother to us in the order of grace" (cf. ibid.), the Council stresses that her spiritual motherhood is not limited to the disciples alone, as though the words spoken by Jesus on Calvary: "Woman, behold your son" (Jn 19:26), required a restrictive interpretation. Indeed, with these words the Crucified One established an intimate relationship between Mary and his beloved disciple, a typological figure of universal scope, intending to offer his Mother as Mother to all mankind.

On the other hand, the universal efficacy of the redeeming sacrifice and Mary's conscious co-operation with Christ's sacrificial offering does not allow any limitation of her motherly love.

Mary's universal mission is exercised in the context of her unique relationship with the Church. With her concern for every Christian, and indeed for every human creature, she guides the faith of the Church towards an ever deeper acceptance of God's Word, sustains her hope, enlivens her charity and fraternal communion and encourages her apostolic dynamism.

3. During her earthly life, Mary showed her spiritual motherhood to the Church for a very short time. Nonetheless, the full value of her role appeared after the Assumption and is destined to extend down the centuries to the end of the world. The Council expressly states: "This motherhood of Mary in the order of grace continues uninterruptedly from the consent which she gave in faith at the Annunciation and which she sustained without wavering beneath the Cross, until the eternal fulfillment of all the elect" (*Lumen gentium*, n.62).

Having entered the Father's eternal kingdom, closer to her divine Son and thus closer to us all, she can more effectively exercise in the Spirit the role of maternal intercession entrusted to her by divine Providence.

4. The heavenly Father wanted to place Mary close to Christ and in communion with him who can "save those who draw near to God through him, since

he always lives to make intercession for them" (Heb 7:25): he wanted to unite to the Redeemer's intercession as a priest that of the Blessed Virgin as a mother. It is a role she carries out for the sake of those who are in danger and in need of temporal favours and, especially, eternal salvation: "By her maternal charity, she cares for the brethren of her Son, who still journey on the earth surrounded by danger and difficulties, until they are led into their blessed home. Therefore the Blessed Virgin is invoked in the Church under the titles of Advocate, Helper, Benefactress, and Mediatrix" (*Lumen gentium*, n.62).

These titles, suggested by the faith of the Christian people, help us to better understand the nature of the Mother of the Lord's intervention in the life of the Church and of the individual believer.

5. The title "Advocate" goes back to St. Irenaeus. With regard to Eve's disobedience and Mary's obedience, he says that at the moment of the Annunciation "the Virgin Mary became the Advocate" of Eve (*Haer*. 5,19,1; *PG* 7, 1175-1176). In fact, with her "yes" she defended our first mother and freed her from the consequences of her disobedience, becoming the cause of salvation for her and the whole human race.

Mary exercises her role as "Advocate" by co-operating both with the Spirit the Paraclete and with the One who interceded on the Cross for his persecutors (cf. Lk 23:34), whom John calls our "advocate with the Father" (1 Jn 2:1). As a mother, she defends her children and protects them from the harm caused by their own sins.

Mary is close to those suffering or in danger

Christians call upon Mary as "Helper," recognizing her motherly love which sees her children's needs and is ready to come to their aid, especially when their eternal salvation is at stake.

The conviction that Mary is close to those who are suffering or in situations of serious danger has prompted the faithful to invoke her as "Benefactress". The same trusting certainty is expressed in the most ancient Marian prayer with the words: "We fly to thy patronage, O holy Mother of God; despise not our petitions in our necessities but deliver us always from all dangers, O glorious and blessed Virgin" (from the *Roman Breviary*).

As maternal Mediatrix, Mary presents our desires and petitions to Christ, and transmits the divine gifts to us, interceding continually on our behalf.

Reprinted from *L'Osservatore Romano*, English Edition.

N.41   L'OSSERVATORE ROMANO   Weekly Edition 11

Mary Mediatrix

"Far from being an obstacle to the exercise of Christ's unique mediation, Mary instead highlights its fruitfulness and efficacy," the Holy Father said at the General Audience of Wednesday, 1 October. In his talk, the Pope fo-

cused on Mary's role as "Mediatrix," which derives from Christ's and in no way overshadows it. Here is a translation of his catechesis, which was the 65th in the series on the Blessed Mother and was given in Italian.

1. Among the titles attributed to Mary in the Church's devotion, chapter eight of *Lumen gentium* recalls that of "Mediatrix". Although some Council Fathers did not fully agree with this choice of title (cf. *Acta Synodalia* III, 8, 163-164), it was nevertheless inserted into the Dogmatic Constitution on the Church as confirmation of the value of the truth it expresses. Care was therefore taken not to associate it with any particular theology of mediation, but merely to list it among Mary's other recognized titles.

Moreover the conciliar text had already described the meaning of the title "Mediatrix" when it said that Mary "by her manifold intercession continues to bring us the gifts of eternal salvation" (*Lumen gentium*, n.62).

As I recalled in my Encyclical *Redemptoris Mater*; "Mary's mediation is intimately linked with her motherhood. It possesses a specifically maternal character, which distinguishes it from the mediation of the other creatures" (n.38).

From this point of view it is unique in its kind and singularly effective.

Mediation of Christ is not obscured by Mary's

2. With regard to the objections made by some of the Council Fathers concerning the term "Mediatrix,"

the Council itself provided an answer by saying that Mary is "a mother to us in the order of grace" (*Lumen gentium*, n.61). We recall that Mary's mediation is essentially defined by her divine motherhood. Recognition of her role as mediatrix is moreover implicit in the expression "our Mother," which presents the doctrine of Marian mediation by putting the accent on her motherhood. Lastly, the title "Mother in the order of grace" explains that the Blessed Virgin co-operates with Christ in humanity's spiritual rebirth.

3. Mary's maternal mediation does not obscure the unique and perfect mediation of Christ. Indeed, after calling Mary "Mediatrix," the Council is careful to explain that this "neither takes away anything from nor adds anything to the dignity and efficacy of Christ the one Mediator" (*Lumen gentium*, n.62). And on this subject it quotes the famous text from the First Letter to Timothy: "For there is one God and there is one mediator between God and men, the man Christ Jesus, who gave himself as a ransom for all" (2:5-6).

In addition, the Council states that "Mary's function as Mother of men in no way obscures or diminishes this unique mediation of Christ, but rather shows its power (*Lumen gentium*, n.60).

Therefore, far from being an obstacle to the exercise of Christ's unique mediation, Mary instead highlights its fruitfulness and efficacy. "The Blessed Virgin's salutary influence on men originates not in any inner necessity but in the disposition of God. It flows forth from the superabundance of the merits of

Christ, rests on his mediation, depends entirely on it and draws all its power from it" (*Lumen gentium*, n.60).

4. The value of Mary's mediation derives from Christ and thus the salutary influence of the Blessed Virgin "does not hinder in any way the immediate union of the faithful with Christ but on the contrary fosters it" (ibid.).

The intrinsic orientation to Christ of the "Mediatrix's" work spurred the Council to recommend that the faithful turn to Mary "so that, encouraged by this maternal help they may the more closely adhere to the Mediator and Redeemer" (*Lumen gentium*, n.62).

In proclaiming Christ the one mediator (cf. 1 Tim 2:5-6), the text of St. Paul's Letter to Timothy excludes any other parallel mediation, but not subordinate mediation. In fact, before emphasizing the one exclusive mediation of Christ, the author urges "that supplications, prayers, intercessions and thanksgivings be made for all men" (2:1). Are not prayers a form of mediation? Indeed, according to St. Paul, the unique mediation of Christ is meant to encourage other dependent, ministerial forms of mediation. By proclaiming the uniqueness of Christ's mediation, the Apostle intends only to exclude any autonomous or rival mediation, and not other forms compatible with the infinite value of the Saviour's work.

5. It is possible to participate in Christ's mediation in various areas of the work of salvation. After stressing that "no creature could ever be counted

along with the Incarnate Word and Redeemer" (n.62), *Lumen gentium* describes how it is possible for creatures to exercise certain forms of mediation which are dependent on Christ. In fact, "just as the priesthood of Christ is shared in various ways both by his ministers and the faithful, and as the one goodness of God is radiated in different ways among his creatures, so also the unique mediation of the Redeemer does not exclude but rather gives rise to a manifold co-operation which is but a sharing in this one source" (*Lumen gentium*, n.62).

Mary's maternal role depends on Christ's mediation

This desire to bring about various participations in the one mediation of Christ reveals the gratuitous love of God who wants to share what he possesses.

6. In truth, what is Mary's maternal mediation if not the Father's gift to humanity? This is why the Council concludes: "The Church does not hesitate to profess this subordinate role of Mary, which it constantly experiences and recommends to the heartfelt attention of the faithful" (ibid.).

Mary carries out her maternal role in constant dependence on the mediation of Christ and from him receives all that his heart wishes to give mankind.

On her earthly pilgrimage the Church "continuously" experiences the effective action of her "Mother in the order of grace."

Reprinted from *L'Osservatore Romano,* English Edition.

Appendix III